The Lord commanded Joshua, saying,

"Take for yourselves twelve men from the people,
    one man from each tribe, and command them, saying,
    'Take up for yourselves twelve stones
    from out in the middle of the Jordan,
    from the place where the priests' feet are standing firm,
    and carry them over with you,
    and lay them down in the lodging place
    where you will lodge tonight...
...let this be a sign among you,
    so that when your children ask later, saying,
    'What do these stones mean to you?'
    then you shall say to them,
    'Because the waters of the Jordan
    were cut off before the Ark of the Covenant of the Lord;
    when it crossed the Jordan,
    the waters of the Jordan were cut off.'
    So these stones shall become a memorial
    to the people of Israel forever."

"...So that all the peoples of the earth
    may know that the hand of the Lord is mighty,
    so that you may fear the Lord your God forever."

— *Joshua 4: 4-6, 24*

STONES IN THE RIVER

ISBN 978-0-692-08081-8

First edition.

Printed in the U.S.A.

© 2018 by Jo King Jackson

Editor: Bill Blankschaen | StoryBuilders

Book Design: Margarita Capella Solazzo | Capella+Solazzo Design

Photographer: Brook Todd | Brook Todd Photography

STONES IN THE RIVER

Discovering Your Spiritual Markers of God's Love, Grace, and Faithfulness

JO KING JACKSON

BROOK TODD PHOTOGRAPHY

IN HIS NAME

STEVE + SUE DON + JO STEVE + SHANNON JAKE ZACKARY PAYTON QUINN BRANDON + MEGHAN MADELINE CATHERINE ABIGAIL BECKHAM ZOEY LOGAN LUCAS JACKSON JONAS RYAN + JULIE JOSHUA GRACE NOAH GABRIELLE SOPHIA HUDSON STEPHEN + HANNAH ROBERT + SARAH ABIGAIL RACHAEL SAMUEL + HANNAH JOSEPH + REBECCA

To my beloved husband, Don,
thank you for your love, encouragement, support, and obedience
to the shared calling that God placed on our lives
to write His Story of Faithfulness.

To our 10 children, 22 grandchildren, and 2 great-grandchildren,
if it were not for each of you, our river of life would have no song.
Like stones in our lives and the river of love that runs through our family,
each of you is remarkable and exceptional,
holding a treasured place in our hearts.

Every page is written with sifted memories in my mind
and gathered from the very center of my soul.
You have all contributed to this beautiful story.

This entire book is my dedication of love for you…
every detail, every photo, every word.
How blessed we are to be born into this circle of love,
at the center of which, is GOD.

TABLE OF CONTENTS

Foreword by Joni Eareckson Tada..............8

Join Me in the Bunkroom 11

Stones and Spiritual Markers..............17

STONE 1   *Foundations of Faith and Family*..............27

STONE 2   *Friendship, Faith, and False Starts*..............45

STONE 3   *Life without a Compass*..............59

STONE 4   *Marriage*..............77

STONE 5   *Motherhood*..............105

STONE 6   *Seasons of Friendship*..............143

STONE 7   *Desert Journeys*..............165

STONE 8   *Grief and Loss*..............187

STONE 9   *Surrender and Renewal*..............207

STONE 10 *Blessing and Favor*..............227

STONE 11 *Garlands of Grace*..............265

STONE 12 *A Fresh Calling*..............315

Living Your Spiritual Legacy..............347

My Special Thanks..............356

Resources..............358

About the Author..............359

BEFORE YOU BEGIN...

What do you do with those rare, golden moments of life when you are swept into wonder or when joy bubbles up in your heart like an artesian spring? How do you contain such heart-stopping moments before they slip through the fingers of time? You cannot. But, you can savor them. You can humbly thank God for them. And if you are like my friend Jo King Jackson, you can write about them.

It's the best you can do. When life's finest moments spring upon you — when your spirit soars after a delightful fireside evening with family and friends, or tears overflow when your daughter calls you her dearest friend — you do all you can to hold onto the ethereal moment, but you cannot. And so, before that deep, unspeakable, joyous memory disappears like stardust, you quickly grab a pen to write it down, as if putting the transcendent onto paper. We can't cling to moments and memories, but we can try our best to capture the feel and flavor, the lingering delight and the lesson learned.

I have a friend who experienced this on his first raft trip down a wild river in the remote back country of Oregon. As the raft swept along in the rapid current, he would fill his eyes with a rugged vista unlike anything he had ever seen. Keeping his eyes pinned on the massive cliffs, he would soon find himself facing sideways and then backwards as the beautiful tableau swept by. But facing backwards to see what was now departing behind him, he realized that he was missing the next beautiful scene around the next bend in the river.

He couldn't stop the river. He couldn't freeze the moment. But he, too, was able to pick up a pen and pour out on paper the treasure trove of insights gleaned from his day on the river. And his journal became a shaft of light, helping others see and experience what touched his heart that day on the water beneath the towering cliffs.

Jo King Jackson has done the same in her stunning new book, Stones in the River.

She has savored and seen much over the years, and like a good steward of time and its gifts, she has captured the celestial moments of her life in this remarkable family journal.

Whether memories from her childhood growing up in the farmland of the Midwest, or carving out a living in California with her rugged, handsome husband by her side, Jo describes each experience as a steppingstone, linking her from one season of life to the next. Drawing from snippets of poems, slivers of scripture, and her personal diaries, Jo gently opens the eyes of her readers, showing them the richness of life in each precious moment. Stones in the River is like a shaft of light – it brightens the possibility of helping us capture our own life lessons to pass on to other generations.

And as you slowly read through its chapters, do not miss the obvious. For there is something celestial written on nearly every page, a greater Story filled with life-lessons that will last you for all of eternity. Jo introduces you to the Author of every sun-kissed memory and every Spirit-filled moment that has broken your heart with His love and beauty. She speaks tenderly of her Lord and Savior, the One who dipped his pen in the ink of every page of her life. Her story is really His Story. Stones in the River just wouldn't be complete without His touch.

So, linger long over the pages of the book you hold in your hands. Do not breeze by the stunning photos or gloss over the images. Savor the life-stories and lessons that Jo King Jackson shares from the depths of her heart. Take up her counsel and pick up a pen and paper, for Jo is (like my river-rafting friend), a sage guide for life-learning, showing us how to wisely weave our own stories not only from the stardust of family memories and times past, but from the brightest Story of them all… the God of the Bible. After all, your life story just wouldn't be complete without His touch.

Joni Eareckson Tada

Joni and Friends International Disability Center, Agoura Hills, California

JOIN ME IN THE BUNKROOM...

Sitting cross-legged on the barn-wood floor of our grandchildren's bunk room one day, I emptied the contents of a crusty, old trunk and found myself surrounded with remnants and reminders of the favorite people, places, experiences, and events of my life—photographs, books, notes, letters, devotionals, and some of my treasured Bibles with scribbling and journaling in the margins. As I gazed thoughtfully over the history of my years, I felt a deep stirring within me. I wondered what value these items could have for my children, grandchildren, and generations to come.

Then Joshua came to mind. His story is one on my favorite Old Testament chronicles of God's covenant of love, faithfulness, and might. After the priests carried the Ark of the Covenant into the Jordan River, God stopped the water's flow so His people could cross without one wet foot.

As I pondered these verses on that barn-wood floor, I began to think, *How can I gather my stones of God's faithfulness in my life to help those whom I love who are coming along after me—my precious children, grandchildren, and great-grandchildren? How can I record the testimony of God's faithfulness to me and our family as indisputable evidence of God's love and care?*

My mind raced as I considered God's hand on my life and pondering all my own "stones" strewn before me on the floor. I shared my excitement with my husband, Don Jackson, that evening after dinner. It all bubbled forth, overflowing with memories of moments in my life when I knew God had designed my path and held His hand upon me. Stories of His faithfulness percolated uncontrollably in my mind.

Don was quick to respond to my enthusiasm. Don and I each had lived a full life prior to meeting. We each had enjoyed long marriages and been blessed with

children and grandchildren, before each of our spouses were diagnosed with terminal illnesses that would demand great faith, courage, and endurance. We had both suffered the pain of loss and the solitary journey of widowhood; but through it all, God was faithful and continued to shower each of us with the laughter of grandbabies between the tears, bringing joy beyond measure. (Our full love story follows in a later chapter!)

So began my study of Joshua's Stones in the River. Following the divine example, I attempted to creatively arrange the wisdom of a lifetime and all of my life experiences in a way that would encourage my family members to create a life of significance and beauty for generations to come on this Journey of Life. Yet as I became excited about recording God's faithfulness in my life, I realized my journey might also help other women who, like me, have experienced love, loss, and life—maybe even you, Dear Reader.

Perhaps like me, you have experienced life with vigor, energy, and enthusiasm and open-handedly received the incredible joy and abundant blessings of God. Perhaps like me, you've learned that life is not lived in a single state of bliss; it can also be a steep climb. Often, we can find ourselves exhausted, discouraged, alone, out of touch, in need of hope, experiencing doubt in ourselves about our capabilities, our worth, or our faith. Perhaps like me, at the tender age of seventy-six, you are still asking the difficult questions of life.

Life is an exciting pilgrimage of faith, discovery, and courage. Ever since I first felt God's call several years ago to write this journey of Stones, I have earnestly prayed for God's Will to be done with this book. I've spent long hours in His Word each day, where I learned more of Him and His ways. I prayed that I would not disappoint Him or be an embarrassment to Him and that you, my

You are an epistle of Christ...
written not with ink
but by the Spirit of the living God,
not on tablets of stone
but on tablets of flesh, that is,
of the heart.

— 2 Corinthians 3:3

dear child of the King, will see Him woven into the very woof and warp of these pages—into every fiber of your life. He loves and cares for you as your Abba Father, going before and beside you each step of the way, day after day, from here to eternity.

My husband and family have inspired me in recording these Stones as have many friends along the way, from my spiritual mentors, to my prayer sisters of thirty-five years, and to my covenant sisters with whom I share life today. They have affirmed that God has given me this pen to share His truths. The women with whom I have shared these Stones while speaking at events have urged me to write down these lessons, sharing God's wisdom, words, and warnings. They tell me how they are hurting, lost, and in need of God's guidance. When speaking to a group of women, the Lord so sharpens my sensory antennae that it's as if I almost hear their hearts crying for a safe place to rest. Jesus is the answer to everything.

I have prayed these many months of writing, while spending days of sunshine in the bunkroom, that the Lord would use this book to call back to others on this pilgrimage, cheerily beckoning them to keep going and keep climbing, reaching back and lending a hand in their climb. It's what we are all called to do, isn't it—no matter where we are on the journey? I thank God and pray for all those women who've called back to me in my life— my grandmother, my mother, my aunts, my spiritual mentors, my prayer sisters, my teachers, and my daughters who are so much wiser and better grounded than I was at their age.

I pray this book blesses you! I pray that through it, the Holy Spirit teaches you, inspires you, and encourages you to identify your own Stones in the River of God's love, grace, and faithfulness while you are building your Spiritual Family Legacy.

In His world, we are all on this journey together.

Love and Blessings,

As you come to Him, a living stone rejected by men
but in the sight of God chosen and precious,
you yourselves like living stones are being built up
as a spiritual house, to be a holy priesthood,
to offer spiritual sacrifices acceptable to God
through Jesus Christ.

— 1 Peter 2:4-5

STONES & SPIRITUAL MARKERS

*A*s we begin to make this journey through Stones in the River, allow me to ask a question: What stones will be the spiritual markers found in your river of life? Are they stepping stones, taking you from one point to another? Are they building stones, to grow and encourage you? Are they foundational truth stones you can build your life on? Or are they stones you repeatedly stumble over, such as the lies Satan whispers in our ears? Might they be stones that weigh you down—discouragement, discontent, and doubt, hanging like millstones around your neck?

These stones begin as small pebbles, often hardly noticed at the time, as they are tossed and turned in life's churning currents. Yet God takes these stones and makes them into beautiful, lasting, and significant markers that define who we become— lovingly fashioned by the hand of God. He is, after all, the Rock who serves as the very cornerstone of our lives. He sends streams of living water over our stones— washing, cleansing, and smoothing them to be used for good in our lives. Through faith in Jesus, we become stones of a different sort, Living Stones that contribute to the building of His beautiful Spiritual House.

Spiritual Markers identify a time of transition, a point of decision, or a season of change when we know God directed us according to His divine purpose, although it may be years before we see it was His hand at work. The Book of Joshua describes how God asked the people to make a memorial of Stones so they would remember His mighty and faithful hand. God did not want His actions for His people to remain hidden. He intended for future generations to learn of His faithfulness and power from the stones set in place by their parents. The stones in the river were Spiritual Markers for the Israelites, reminding them of life-altering events God did not want them to forget.

Spiritual Markers commemorate an encounter of some sort with God. They can signify a decision we made, such as when we heard God's call and surrendered all to follow Christ. They can also be connected to God's intervention, such as a close brush with death. When I was a young mother of two, my husband and I were driving in the fast lane of the freeway when we saw all the cars in front of us quickly veering into the right lane. In an instant, we came face-to-face with a black car speeding towards us going the wrong direction. Somehow we swerved out of the way without hitting any cars in the next lane. Later, we heard on the news that the driver, intending suicide, died after hitting a family of five head-on. They were seriously injured, but survived.

I didn't fully recover from that experience for a long time. Both my husband and I later recalled feeling pushed out of the way. We knew God had spared our lives. That moment became a spiritual marker of God's saving Providence. I kept a small black toy car in a Shadow Box display to remind me of God's intervention. God called me to make Him a greater priority in my life.

These Spiritual Markers can be memorials of God's activity. The event or experience may feel either good or bad, but we come to see how it shapes our lives for good over time. After losing my husband (also named Don) to cancer in 2001, I prayed daily for God's guidance in my life. I was employed full time then with a career I loved, but I sensed an urgency to change my life direction. When God prepares you for a new direction in life, He often takes you aside, as it were, to provide a time for soul-searching of that restlessness within your spirit. Each time you encounter God's call or His new direction, you find a spiritual marker.

In 2004, God gave me an unrelenting restlessness within my spirit. I was introduced to a women's study, The Master's Program for Women. It was designed to help guide women from success to significance in all realms of life—the Personal

Realm, the Family Realm and the Kingdom Realm, using our gifts and talents to make a difference in serving others in God's Kingdom. We had twelve quarterly meetings over a three-year period, studying in our workbooks between meetings, focusing on change from the inside out.

After doing my written homework for the first month, I recognized a problem. I discovered my Life Ladder was leaning against the wrong building! I was working seventy hours a week, making a wonderful salary, meeting wonderful people, and serving God in my work environment—but I knew God was calling me out of the secular work realm to be fully available to Him for His plan for my life. He began revealing His truths to me. Little by little, He repositioned my priorities and removed all desires of career or financial stability.

I had an unquenchable thirst for one thing: to be in His will for my life. Little did I know where He was going to take me! He brought another Don, Don Jackson, into my life. Seven weeks later, we were married and living in Kingsburg, California, four hours away from my home of forty years in Southern California. I felt His call to change the direction of my life, saying, "Come with Me, Jo! Give up everything and come with Me!" Only God could have prepared my heart to follow Don to our new home and family. I knew where I had come from, but God knew where He wanted me to go.

God was faithful! My first three years in Kingsburg were meant to give me the time and treasure of drawing close to Him, studying His Word, and learning of Him. I prayed day and night that God would show me His purpose for my days that were ordained by Him. Don and I spent the first two or three years bringing our families together—five married children and twenty-two grandchildren. As we watched our grandchildren grow, Don and I began talking about our family legacy and reflecting on spiritual markers.

BIBLE MARGIN: 2009

"Oh, Lord, that you may, indeed, incline my heart to you,
that I may walk in your ways, keep your Commandments
and your Statutes and your Precepts!"

WHY ARE SPIRITUAL MARKERS IMPORTANT?

Some markers are meant to be shared, to pass on to our children and grandchildren. As we share our stories with each other, they become a spiritual marker that points people to God's activity in their own lives. Our spiritual markers provide an opportunity to teach our children and grandchildren about how God works in our lives and on our behalf as our caring, loving Father. I loved hearing the stories my grandmother told of struggles during the Great Depression. God provided for her when she was widowed at an early age with five young children. Even though I knew most of her stories by heart, I always enjoyed hearing her tell them again. I loved hearing my father sharing what it was like, as the oldest of those five siblings, to have to leave school after the third grade to help provide for all of the family. God always provided a place to work and earn money, often with fatherly love and guidance as an extra bonus. He always gave glory to God for raising him from faraway in heaven. Those spiritual markers, passed on to me from generations before, gave me hope during life's difficulties.

In 2009, I believed God was calling me to write down some spiritual markers of my life—the day I referred to earlier in my opening note, when I had emptied the contents of my old trunk on the barn-wood floor. His call to me was to write a book of His profound love and faithfulness. He wanted me to testify to the truth of how intent He is on taking us all from where we are and bringing us into an intimate, close relationship with Him, building our character, making and molding us more like Him everyday.

The steps of a good man are ordered by the Lord,
And He delights in his way....
....The law of his God is in his heart; None of his steps shall slide.

— Psalm 37:23, 31

Then Samuel took a stone and set it between
Mizpah and Shen, and named it Ebenezer,
saying, "Thus far the Lord has helped us."

— 1 Samuel 7:12

He is making, breaking, and blessing us to give to others and prepare us for life with Him in eternity. He sets us apart for Him and calls us to higher ground, to intentionally leave the legacy of the Lord's Story for our children, grandchildren, and generations to follow. Our spiritual markers provide the opportunity to teach our children about how God works in our lives and on our behalf as our Divine Advocate and Abba Father.

"Truth is not discovered; it is revealed."

— Experiencing God,
Henry & Richard Blackaby, pg. 72

"You cannot stay where you are and go with God at the same time!"

— Experiencing God,
Henry & Richard Blackaby, pg. 60

"Our Spiritual Markers develop our character...lean on Him."

— Experiencing God,
Henry & Richard Blackaby

Spiritual markers strengthen our own relationship with God. Remembrance of our spiritual markers leads to gratitude for the past, assurance in the present, and hope for our future. Over time, I can look back at these markers and see how God has so faithfully directed, intervened, and changed the course of my life, according to His Divine Purpose.

Spiritual markers also point others to God. We are meant to be a living testimony to the Lord. Think of all the people you meet every day who are hungry for answers but don't even know the questions to ask. When we share our lives with them, drawing a circle lovingly around them to invite them in, God can use these times to capture their hearts in a profound way. It may be the mere planting of a seed, a watering of a young sprout, or the harvesting of ripe fruit. What a blessing it is to be His hands with His gentle touch and His mouth to affirm His Love! Our time on earth is so short, Dear Reader. We need to be about our Father's business each and every day, suiting up and showing up for whomever God sends our way in His Divine Appointments. It's never about *what*, but always about *who*.

And my God shall supply all your needs according to His riches in glory by Jesus Christ.

— Philippians 4:19

WHAT ARE YOUR SPIRITUAL MARKERS?

You may want to begin keeping a spiritual journal as we journey together exploring the twelve significant stones that I think most women experience throughout life in some form or another. It will be good to record the times God has revealed a Truth to you or to jot down things God has said to you in prayer time and things He is saying while reading His Word. This practice will help when developing your own Spiritual Family Legacy.

- Look back on your Christian life and list ways in which God has been faithful to you, guided you, intervened in your plans, etc.
- What have been some markers that shaped the direction of your life?
- Was there a time you realized you needed salvation and gave your life to Christ?
- Who are some of the mentors in your life who brought you closer to God?
- Do you sense there is far more that God wants to do through your life than what you have been experiencing? Ask God to show you, then be prepared to respond in faith and obedience!

As the Spirit of the Lord works in us,
we become more and more like Him
and reflect His Glory even more.

— *2 Corinthians 3:19*

STONE 1   FOUNDATIONS OF FAITH AND FAMILY

I'll never forget the first time I saw Him. The sun was shining brightly through the windows of St. Robert's Catholic Church, illuminating all the dust particles dancing in the air. I followed the white rays of sunshine to the front altar. There He was, arms stretched out with His feet crossed at the bottom. My knees rested gently on a padded kneeler alongside my father, three half-sisters, and stepmother.

As I slowly turned my head to get my stepmother's attention, I saw she had already seen Him. With her chin gently leaning on her folded hands, eyes closed, she silently moved her lips as I had seen her do so many mornings beside her bed. Now, as I saw her absorbed in prayer, I had an urgent need to know what she was saying to Him. I made a mental note to ask her as soon as we got home.

HIS CALLING : TEACH ME TO PRAY

We always stopped at Palmer's Delicatessen for hard rolls and cream cheese on the way home from church. My father was a friend of Mr. Palmer and loyal to other small business owners, so he liked to give him our business every Sunday. After church and Palmer's Deli, we set about our routine duties. We all knew our assignments. My father would retreat to his favorite overstuffed chair to read the Sunday edition of The Milwaukee Journal while drinking his black coffee—the stronger the better. My father worked hard six days a week at his piano and organ store in downtown

Milwaukee. They were closed on Sundays like most stores in those "good ol' days," and families spent the day together.

My brother went outside with his friends while my sisters and I helped Mom in the kitchen. We squeezed Valencia oranges by hand, sending up the most wonderful fragrance. Since butter was a luxury, we bought Blue Bonnet Margarine. A button in the center of the brick-sized, plastic pocket was filled with margaric crystals. The best Sunday assignment of all was popping the margarine button and massaging the red crystals into the white lard until it was all blended into a soft, smooth, beautiful buttercup yellow. It took as long to work the margarine from white to buttercup yellow as it did to prepare the entire breakfast! Eggs were fried, bacon was browned, and the hard rolls came out of the oven warmed and ready to butter. My stepmom made a game of teaching us how we could have everything arrive hot on the table at the same time. She called it "the art of cooking."

Finally, when we were all seated and prayer was offered, we dove into our feast. I talked first before anyone else could empty their mouths. "Mom," I said, "when you're in church and you see Jesus on the cross, you always talk to Him for a long time. Sometimes I see you in your bedroom, and your eyes are closed and your lips are moving the same way. What do you say to Him? Does He hear you? Does He answer you?"

Pausing for a moment, she looked at my dad and smiled. Then, putting down her fork, she leaned forward and said the most amazing thing. "Honey, the Jesus you see on the cross is only a reminder of our Sweet Savior who lives in our heart. He is with us all the time, day in and day out, in sunshine and in rain. When we talk to Him in prayer, thanking Him for our family, our home, our food, our friends, He listens and hears. God is love, Joanne, and He loves us and

My brother Jim and me

cares for us. We can talk to Him anytime, anywhere, because He lives in our heart. You can ask Him to come into your heart, too, and He will come in and live with you forever."

My eyes stayed open, but my mind was back at the altar of St. Robert's, remembering Jesus on the cross, thinking of all the things I would say to Him if I really knew He would listen and hear me. I sat silently, utterly amazed. I don't remember the rest of the meal. My head was spinning with excitement.

I spent the rest of the day outside with my brother and sisters. My brother walked us a few blocks down to the outdoor ice-skating rink, where they hosed and froze over a section of the playground every winter. Everyone was there, including my soon-to-be best friend, Marline. We put on our freshly polished white ice skates with cold, stiff fingers, tightening our laces as we laughed, quickly joining into the circle of friends on the rink. Our favorite game was "Crack the Whip." One player, chosen as head of the whip, skated around in a circle with other players quickly skating to catch the hand of the person at the tail. The more people, the longer the tail, and the faster and further it circled, making it difficult to catch, much less hold onto, the hand of the last skater at the tail. It was all pure fun and an exhausting experience.

When our toes were almost frozen, we ran quickly into the Shanty House to warm ourselves around the potbelly stove. Homemade hot chocolate with marshmallows on top would leave a residue of warmth and comfort in our tummies. We skated and took Shanty breaks until the streetlights came on, then headed home.

That night, as I lay in my bed, snuggled between my warm flannel sheets under mounds of blankets, I carefully went over everything my stepmother had told me that morning. I think I stopped breathing as I imagined what it would be like to have Jesus live in my heart. With all the trust of my heart, I quietly slipped out of bed onto the cold, bare floor.

There on my knees, I closed my eyes, gently leaning my chin on my folded hands just as I had seen Mom do, and said, "Oh, dear sweet Jesus, please come into my heart and live with me forever and ever. I can only think of one thing I want…would you please, please, please teach me to pray?"

I quickly jumped back into my bed, shivering and smiling as though I had just discovered a big, wonderful secret. I wondered if He had, indeed, heard me! As I glanced out my window into the wintry, white, snowy Wisconsin night, my heart was warm. I knew I wasn't alone. The cornerstone of my spiritual legacy had been laid in my heart.

Your faith in Christ is your spiritual cornerstone. Building your spiritual foundation begins with a simple faith in Christ.

My maternal grandparents
William and Catherine Voysey

OUR FOUNDATION OF FAITH

I met a woman the other day whose sad and downcast eyes made a melancholy contrast with her smiling face. She had been widowed ten months earlier after being married for over forty-three years to her high-school sweetheart. Her children were grown and busy with their lives, leaving her "alone, afraid, confused and without hope." I realized this was a divine appointment as she said, "I don't know what to do; I have no faith. I was never raised with faith. My parents had no faith."

Our foundations of faith are laid early in life. Each of us is created to know God (John 3:17). We are created to know and love Him, to have fellowship and intimacy with Him, and to serve His Kingdom and His people here on earth. We are created with a hole in our hearts that only He can fill, and our souls are not at rest until we rest in Him (Psalm 62:1). We were not created for this world, but rather for eternity.

We were created to be God-centered, not self-centered. Through our fellowship with Him and reading His Word, God develops our character into His likeness. Our time on earth is designed to build and strengthen our character until we arrive home with Him in Heaven. On this lifelong journey, the more we know God, the more our faith grows. The more our faith grows, the more we come to believe in His love and trust in His care for us.

As the spirit of the Lord works in us,
we become more and more like Him
and reflect His Glory even more.

— 2 Corinthians 3:19

My divine appointment with that grieving soul was an example of God's loving and gentle touch when we are open to His plan for our day. Our faithful God intervened

HOW TO KNOW GOD PERSONALLY

Created by Campus Crusade

PRINCIPLE 1 God loves you and offers a wonderful plan for your life.

*God so loved the world that He gave His one and only Son,
that whoever believes in Him shall not perish, but have eternal life.*
— *John 3:16*

PRINCIPLE 2 All of us sin and our sin has separated us from God.

All have sinned and fall short of the glory of God.
— *Romans 3:23*

PRINCIPLE 3 Jesus Christ is God's only provision for our sin. Through Him we can know and experience God's love and plan for our life.

*God demonstrates His own love toward us,
in that while we were yet sinners, Christ died for us.*
— *Romans 5:8*

PRINCIPLE 4 We must individually receive Jesus Christ as Savior and Lord; then we can know and experience God's love and plan for our lives.

*As many as received Him, to them He gave the right to
become children of God, even to those who believe in His name.*

— *John 1:12*

so that our paths crossed while standing side-by-side in the checkout lane at the local grocery. I had three or four more urgent errands to run before catching a plane, but from former experiences of hearing His gentle nudge, I knew that my only important assignment at that moment was to be fully present right where I was.

I was drawn into the beautiful spirit of this hurting woman, no longer a stranger as God intertwined our hearts. For the next forty minutes, she shared the grief and fear of being alone for the first time in her life. The grief I had experienced myself after losing my husband fifteen years earlier came back to me and fresh tears filled both our eyes.

"I don't know how I can be crying so hard with a total stranger," she said. "I'm so sorry." I paused a moment and asked the Holy Spirit to give me His words for her. I knew that this was an opportunity to bless another through the blessing God had given me. As the Scriptures say, we ourselves are comforted by God so we will be able to comfort those who are in any affliction" (2 Corinthians 1:4).

"God is near the brokenhearted," I gently responded. "He has been beside you all along. Our meeting today was ordained by Him. May I pray with you?"

"Oh, yes, please!"

As our arms enfolded one another, I prayed, "Dear God, would you please send your messenger to come alongside this woman to speak of Your love and protection for her? Replace her fear with a strong and mighty faith in you." As we parted, she promised she would "be on the lookout" every day to see who God would send.

One day, she will look back on that day and know that God touched her in that moment. God uses us every day if we "suit up and show up" to do His

work—to be His eyes to notice our surroundings, His ears to listen between the lines, His lips to speak His words of understanding and love, and His arms to wrap around hurting souls. I was blessed as I prayed with her in the middle of the store on a busy day. You see, I had just begun writing this chapter about the importance of the first stone—a strong foundation of faith and family. As she confided in me that her parents had no faith, God gave me a poignant, personal reminder of how priceless the gift of faith is when we receive it at a young age. The foundations of faith and family stay with us and shape our lives.

- Did you have hope given to you in your early family life?
- What were your early "plantings" of faith?
- Did you hear the words of faith given to you by your mother or father?
- What are your earliest memories of knowing that God had bestowed upon you the gift of faith?

HIS PRESENCE : OUR STORIES

As we begin to revisit our Foundation of Faith and Family as the first Stone in the river of life, let's give thought to the first seedlings so gently planted with God's love and faithfulness. Let us stoop down, and gently sifting through our early waters, pick up some pebbles in the river, and reflect on our heritage of faith.

We treasure a mother or grandmother's secret family recipe, asking her how she makes it and watching her step-by-step as she prepares it. How much more important it is for us, as mothers and grandmothers, to preserve the legacy of faith entrusted to us! God intends for every generation to share with the next generation His mighty acts, faithfulness, and love. In the sharing of our story, we give wings to God's Word. By sharing our faith experiences, we give feet to the story of our personal journey so our children may know about what God has done.

Faith is built at home with every loving gesture that teaches us to express our faith, heart-to-heart with those we love. As we share our stories of the ways the Lord has helped us face challenges and crises in our lives, we encourage one another and give honor and glory to Him. These times when we witness the power and faithfulness of God intervening in our very own lives "gives us a future and a hope" and grows our faith (Jeremiah 29:11).

And now, just as you accepted Christ Jesus, your Lord,
you must continue to follow Him.
Let your roots grow down into Him and let your lives be built on Him.
Then your faith will grow strong in the truth you were taught
and you will overflow with thankfulness.

— Colossians 2:6-7

I'd like to share a story of a young girl. Her parents were divorced when she was just eighteen months old. She lived with her mother and older brother on a beautiful lake in Wisconsin, close to aunts, uncles and cousins she adored. As she grew older, her mother remarried. They moved to Pennsylvania, far away from family, including her brother who was left behind with his dad. As only a faithful Father would do, God moved them next door to a wonderful family who had twin boys the same age as the girl. The three of them spent many wonderful summer days fishing and exploring the outdoors together. She observed the love and traditions of the neighbors' family times, tucking them away in her heart.

Many nights during the three years she lived there with her mother, she would hide under her bed at night, covering her head with pillows so she couldn't hear the

"Life is a succession of lessons which must be lived to be understood."

— *Helen Keller*

loud arguments between her mother and stepdad. Alone under her bed, she cried out to God, whom she had heard about the few times she went to church with her friends. She felt the love, comfort, and calm that came over her when she softly cried for help. It wasn't until she was entering the 7th grade that her mother would once again divorce, allowing them to return to Wisconsin and be near family. Through this too, God was so faithful to her. He heard her cries and comforted her. He always had His hand on her.

How do I know? Because I was that young girl. God brought us back to Wisconsin to set my feet on solid ground. I was so grateful to live close to my dad and family again. My mother and I moved just blocks away from my father, stepmom and half-sisters. Since my mother worked full-time, I spent after-school hours at my dad's house.

I was fortunate to have a stepmother who expressed a deep and abiding faith in Jesus Christ. My dad and stepmom began taking me to church every Sunday. I came to see in later years that God brought me back to my Wisconsin home, because He intended to plant in me the seeds of faith and belief in Him.

HIS BLESSING : SHAPED BY FAMILY

The strongest shaping influence of my faith and values came from watching and listening to my parents and grandparents. My family was large, loving, and loud.

Whether we were sitting around the dinner table, socializing with neighbors, or fellowshipping with our church family, I was always learning. I especially loved the large gatherings where family stories were told from generations back. We stuck together like glue whether times were good or hard. The three principles that shaped my family life were how much we were loved, how hard we worked, and how much was expected of us.

My dad was a strict disciplinarian who passionately wanted to pass on his love for family and a strong work ethic to all five children. He modeled unconditional love, forgiveness, affirmation, encouragement, loyalty, discipline, and obedience. He gave me great resources to survive. From my dad, I caught honesty, perseverance, determination, truthfulness—and stubbornness!

He taught us every Sunday, "A family that prays together, stays together." This was just one of his many dad-isms:

"Keep a stiff upper lip!"

"Pull up your bootstraps and keep going!"

"It isn't over 'til it's over!"

"A man who doesn't work doesn't eat!"

"A penny saved...and given...is a penny saved in Heaven."

"Blessings or curses, the choice is yours, so choose wisely."

My dad also taught us great people skills. We were to be loving and respectful to everyone in our family, but our elders deserved a special portion of honor. Being around older adults gave us ample opportunities for cultivating the art of conversation. Sincere, honest, and strong, he didn't mind disagreements now and then just to keep things interesting. He believed that people didn't care how much you knew until they knew how much you cared—and he lived it out.

My mother backed up the strong work ethic of my dad in the home. She taught me how to cook, clean, and keep a beautiful home. When assigning my chores, she would hide coins in different places—the sofa, chairs, under the bed, and under the toilet bowl (my favorite!). When she came home from work, she asked, "How much money did you earn today?" The more thoroughly I cleaned, the more I made.

My mother was a great and loyal friend to everyone. She was devoted to my brother and me. After she and dad were separated and she was a single mother, she often worked two jobs to provide for us. She had a beautiful voice, so the local radio stations always had a place for her to work in small radio drama and musical shows.

Has anything ever happened in your days
or in the days of your ancestors?
Tell it to your children
and let your children tell it to their children,
and their children to the next generation.

— Joel 1:2-3

My mom remained close to her own parents, and we spent most of our free time with them. I have countless memories of sitting on the front porch on a hot summer's day sipping freshly-squeezed lemonade together. I loved sitting in on their adult conversations of work, friends, and family. Mother was a genius at finding fun things that didn't cost much money. We played games, listened to the radio, loved our Friday-night buttered popcorn, and shared her favorite thing of all: beautiful music. When she wasn't working, beautiful music filled every corner of our home—pop and classical were her favorites. She loved Doris Day and woke me up with a little song every morning:

> *"When the red, red robin comes bob, bob, bobbin' along, along*
> *There'll be no more sobbin' when he starts throbbin' his old sweet song*
> *Wake up, wake up, you sleepy head! Get up, get up, get out of bed.*
> *Cheer up, cheer up, the sun is red. Live, love, laugh, and be happy."*

It was a lovely way to wake up and remains a precious memory even today. Children and grandchildren love to hear these stories of your own childhood over and over again. Don't miss the opportunities to share them. As I reflect on this Stone in the River that represents the foundations of my faith and family, I so clearly see the hand of God guiding my way. How has God gone before you and beside you and behind you in the early years of your life? What are you doing to help shape the character of children God has placed in your life?

I invite you, Dear Reader, to consider your own early story. Esteem and treasure those who helped shape your faith and character. What were the early foundations of faith for you? Have you surrendered your life to Christ? What influences shaped your early beliefs? What lessons did you learn from your parents? Who else set examples of faith for you or prayed for you? As you glance back through your childhood years, gathering, identifying, and naming your faith and family stones, take one step further and place yourself into your children's childhood. How will they cultivate the foundations of faith and family as you leave your spiritual legacy?

My mother Dorothy, my brother Jim, and me

My father Jim

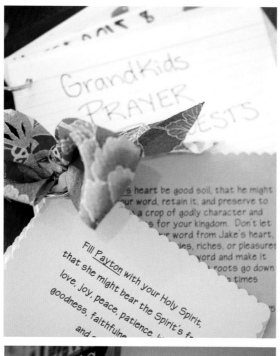

GRACE NOTES | *Foundations of Faith and Family*

- Sometimes we don't know the value of the people who shape our faith or what they have given us until later in life. If they are still living, thank them in person or through a personal note.

- Have your children ask their grandparents to share stories from their childhood.

- Ask for an adult in your family to be the family historian. Find someone who loves taking pictures and chronicling events and family gatherings.

- Record your family ancestry with your elders. Ask them all the questions you can think of. Do it today, while they are still here.

- Make a Family Tree board together, frame it, and place it in a special area in your home.

- Ask a grandparent to recreate stories from their childhood, recording their stories in their own voice.

- Pray the Scriptures for your children and grandchildren. Insert their names in the verses you are praying, personalizing them as you read.

- My children give me "Prayer Rings" with their families' children on index cards. The older ones write what prayers they'd like my husband and I to pray for them. The mothers write requests for the younger children. These are one of my greatest treasures.

- Family Index Cards – Each month I make an index card for:

  1. Birthdays

  2. Praises

  3. Family Needs (one for each family)

  4. My husband and myself

  5. Special Needs (here I name the specific people for whom I have promised to pray when I meet them during my day, plus those friends I cherish who have either asked for prayer or those for whom I believe the Spirit is asking me to pray). Then I rubber-band them and keep them in my Bible or daily devotional. This way I don't let anyone slip through the cracks!

For I know the plans I have for you", declares the Lord,
plans to prosper you and not harm you,
plans to give you hope and a future.

— Jeremiah 29:11

STONE 2   FRIENDSHIP, FAITH, AND FALSE STARTS

*M*y heart swells with gratitude and thankfulness when I think of all our grandchildren and what they are accomplishing with the gifts and talents God has given them. My husband Don and I love spending time with them as they share their joys, adventures, and challenges. We always come away from time with them feeling full of energy and vigor, with a new burst of enthusiasm for life and hope in their bright tomorrows.

Each day with our grandchildren adds another day to our life! Every one of them at every age is so special to us. As my granddaughter and I were walking through a bookstore recently—sharing our mutual love for books—she asked what high school was like for me. Her question took me back to a season of life that, for so many of us, is full of friendships, faith, and false starts.

HIS GUIDANCE : SHOREWOOD HIGH SCHOOL

I entered Shorewood High School with great anticipation. Shorewood was not just any high school—it was one of the most highly esteemed public schools in the nation and it left an indelible mark on my life as a teenager. My teachers became my mentors, building on my family foundation of values. And of course, I made a few life-long friends.

Betsy, Judy, Marline and Sue—I'm sure we had no idea how close we'd become when we first tried out for cheerleading. I jumped into high school with both feet, quickly finding a great group of friends and joining multiple school activities. The squad was comprised of four junior varsity and four senior varsity cheerleaders. At the encouragement of some older students, the four of us tried out for the squad. We all made junior varsity for two years of junior high, and later we all advanced to the varsity squad for four years of high school. Six years on the team formed a friendship that would last our entire lives.

My friends' parents also became part of my family. Though I regret that none of my family members ever came to watch me cheer, many of my friends' parents cheered us onto V-I-C-T-O-R-Y. I learned early on that family and friendships help sustain us through anything life brings our way. Football, basketball, or track, we loved all the athletic seasons. Whether at home or away, we represented our school with pride and honor.

Winter football games in Wisconsin were a challenge. We froze in our short uniforms, but at least we could jump around to keep warm. Halftime found us running across the field to our cheerleader room where big cups of hot chocolate waited. We entertained the visiting cheerleaders, many of whom we grew to know through the years. We cheered for home basketball games in our Shorewood Greyhounds Gym—hot, stinky, and filled to the brim with yelling students and supportive parents. The students anticipated post-game sock-hops nearly as much as the games themselves. We left our shoes outside the door to keep the lacquered floors shiny and clean and danced until they sent us home. The music was loud, and the perspiration ran just as freely as during the game. At the end of the night, we walked home huddled in groups, whether the night was warm or fresh snow crunched beneath our boots. There were no coddling parents waiting for us in the parking lot. We divvied the guys up, two to a group,

My brother Jim and me

and they escorted each of us to our homes. When the temperatures were at their worst, upper classmates would shuttle us home.

Many of those friendships endure to this day, more than fifty years later. And I still love the smell of a stinky basketball gym.

HIS SANCTIFICATION : MY CONVENT SUMMER

In the middle of my high school years, I felt the Lord calling me closer. Since I attended a public high school, I had yet to complete the formal classes required in my Catholic faith. We attended a beautiful church within our close-knit community of Shorewood. The building was encircled with gold-leafed paintings of each Station of the Cross that graced the perimeter columns. Inset stained glass windows depicted different scenes in our Lord's life, from birth to His Ascension into Heaven. Above the entrance were the words of Christ I still remember: "Peace I leave with you; My peace I give to you" (John 14:27).

One spring day, I stopped by the Parish Rectory and inquired about preparation for my Confirmation (which is similar to a Bar Mitzvah in the Jewish faith). It was then I met Father Leahy, who became my spiritual mentor. He faithfully walked me through the Catechism of Instruction, cramming four years of Catholic instruction into two, so I could be confirmed before I graduated high school.

Under Father Leahy's influence, my faith came alive. He taught me how to have a deep, intimate relationship with the Lord and to live my faith "24/7." He would read Scripture aloud to me, close the Bible, and say, "Now Joanne, aren't those the most amazing words you have ever heard? We serve a mighty God." He taught me to dedicate my life to the Lord every morning and how to examine my conscience every evening.

"The morning of your life determines your evening," Father Leahy said. "The beginning of your life determines your ending, Joanne. If you stay close to the Lord, by your life's end you will have become more like Christ as preparation for spending eternity with Him." As I look over the decades of my life now, I can see that he was right: my early years determined my later years. My commitment to finish well burns stronger and brighter than ever. All the trials in the meantime fade away in comparison.

Father Leahy would always end our lessons by sharing a favorite piece of music, whether a great aria from an opera or a beautiful, energetic song from a Broadway show: "Just You Wait, Henry Higgins" from *My Fair Lady* or "Whistle a Happy Tune" from *The King and I*. The music could be heard through the open windows long after I left the rectory.

My thirst for Jesus increased with each instruction. I began going to daily Mass at 6:30 each morning, allowing enough time to walk to school before class. In the quiet, meditative atmosphere of the large-columned sanctuary, I knelt on soft leather kneelers with the aroma of incense gently wafting through the church. I prayed for my family and friends. I prayed for good grades, to be asked to prom, to pass my Shakespeare or Latin exam, and to make Head Cheerleader. Amidst the countless concerns of a high school girl, I also prayed to know Jesus more and become more like Him.

Father Leahy taught me to believe that God had a plan for my life. That plan would not always be easy, but it would always bring great reward, because it was one lived with Him by my side.

St. Robert's Catholic Church,
Shorewood, Wisconsin

THE CALL TO A LIFE OF FAITH

During my senior year, my friend Suzi and I confided to each other that we felt God's call on our life to enter the Convent. Suzi's family agreed to allow her to enter a novitiate after graduation, where she would train prior to making a decision to enter the Convent. I sought out Sr. Honoré at St. Robert's School, where one of my half-sisters attended. She exuded warmth and love. I met with her often, learning about Convent life and the daily discipline required for a lifetime of service to the Lord. She suggested I spend the summer following graduation at the Dominican Mother House in upstate Wisconsin. My father drove me up to the Convent House in early June.

The nun who would oversee me said, "This is a lifetime decision, Joanne, one that must be taken with great seriousness and prayer. You must be in prayer and fasting while you are here, seeking the Lord's will for your life in earnest."

Then Christ will make His home in your hearts
as you trust in Him. Your roots will grow down
into God's love and keep you strong...
so you will know how wide, how long, how high,
and how deep is His love.

— Ephesians 3:17-18

I spent most of my days either with the teaching nuns, with my prayer sister, or in solitude. After early morning prayer and chores, I walked the grounds of the Convent estate along the lake, praying. My evenings were spent in the library—a large room with wood-paneled walls, large worn area rugs, beautiful velvet floral-patterned chairs and sofas, and soft lighting from a fireplace that covered one entire wall. The room was filled with books from floor to ceiling. A ladder on a brass rail, covered in vivid patina from use and age, took one anywhere around the room to reach the desired book. It was simply magnificent.

Despite such idyllic surroundings, I lasted only three weeks! The Lord was quite patient with me. He gently wooed me to an understanding that my great love for Him didn't necessarily mean He must send me either to Africa or the Convent. I could serve Him anywhere and everywhere. Furthermore, He gave me a deep understanding that His primary calling on my life was to be a wife and mother. With a grateful heart, I shared my decision with the Mother Superior. She smiled, took me in her arms and blessed me.

My father wasted no time in retrieving his daughter the next day. We drove home in the heat of a hot, humid July day with the windows rolled down and the dust of the corn harvest blowing in my hair. My dad was quiet as we drove, giving me space to gather my thoughts. After many miles in silence, I began sharing the beautiful experience of my retreat. I told him I felt a profound sense of peace with my decision. My dad wisely said, "Well then, Sweetie, it's time to get on with your life!"

When have you felt the strong hand of God closing a door to a path you thought you were destined to pursue? His guidance often comes by way of shut doors. When He bangs a door closed, we do well to heed His halt. This was, indeed, a spiritual marker in my life, a time of decision when I knew God had clearly guided me.

HIS PRUNING : COLLEGE BOUND

If I wasn't destined for the convent, then I would go to college. I wanted to study for either a nursing or teaching career. Most of my friends were going to the University of Wisconsin, but admission for the next school year was already closed. However, God

*K*now therefore that the Lord your God is God;
He is the faithful God, keeping His covenant of love
to a thousand generations of those
who love Him and keep His commands.

— *Deuteronomy 7:9 NIV*

had put a couple in my life, George and Betty Donovan, who knew the Admissions Director. George drove me to Madison and, before long, I was enrolled in classes and assigned a dorm room with a roommate. Fern was studious but fun, quiet but social—the perfect roommate. She was Jewish, but loved my Catholic self anyway, and I loved her.

Our room housed two tiny beds, two tiny desks, and two tiny closets. One bathroom and one telephone were down the hall. When we had a phone call, the girl on phone duty would yell out our name. We only had five minutes to talk on school nights (imagine!).

My father didn't let me leave home as easily as I'd anticipated. I knew he wanted the best for me. He worked hard all his life and sacrificed a great deal for the love of our family, but college money was not in his plans! He actually offered me a large amount of money (for those days) if I would stay home and get a job. When I didn't accept, he offered me free rent for one year. The next offer was the best, and he was sure it would do the trick: "Sweetie, if you stay home, I'll buy you a brand new Thunderbird car!" I still remember the delighted look on his face when he made this last plea.

I ran over and hugged him as hard as I could, tears running down my face. He would sacrifice the money required for a Thunderbird car, for me! "Oh, Daddy," I said, "there's nothing in the world I'd rather have—not even a Thunderbird—than your help and blessing to go to college!"

He finally relented, after insisting he was just testing me. "Okay, sweetie! Then college it is, but you're going to have to work and go to school at the same time. I'll help the little I can." My father generously paid my tuition and board, and I worked part-time to earn spending money. I was fortunate to get a job in the campus bookstore, along with a discount on textbooks.

I was quite excited to be at such an incredible school. Madison bustled with students, activities, and ideas. There were always things to do or places to go. I loved my classes, though they were far more challenging than I had expected. Sitting in the Zoology lecture hall in my first semester, the professor had us introduce ourselves to the person to the right and the left. Then he said, "One of the three of you will not be here after the first year. Good luck."

I would be the one of those three, but not for academic reasons. My four years of high school and abbreviated Convent Summer had set in place the very backbone of my young adult life. With all that family and friends, teachers and spiritual mentors poured into my life, I cannot help but pause here to point out how faithfully God had ordained my days and prepared me for what was to come.

Believe me, I didn't have it all together. I did not want my high school years to come to an end. I felt far from being prepared to make the transition into young adulthood, let alone "real" adulthood. But I knew that God calls forth the full use of our potential, and I was committed to discovering just what mine was.

Reflect on how God has gone before and beside you—even though you were oblivious to His steps. Who poured into your young life? If you are a young person, who can you seek out to help you now? Who has God placed in your life today that needs your mentoring?

When God places people in our lives who are in need, He already knows what they lack and has given us the resources to meet their needs. When God presents us with a young person to mentor, the best starting question may be, "Who do you want to be, and what can I do to help you succeed?" The answers will tell how we can best be of service to them. They will become better through us, and that, my Dear Reader, is Divine Followership.

As we share the stories of our personal journey, we give wings to God's Word. Our children may know about God and hear about God, but the sharing of our life experiences gives them a real, tangible look at our walk with God.

*My paternal grandmother Lillian
and me with my cousins*

GRACE NOTES | *Friendship, Faith, and False Starts*

- The Lord opens as well as slams doors shut! When in your early years did you run ahead of your parents or God, only to find the doors close? Can you see God's hand on you?

- High School years can be "coming of age" years for some. Reflect on your years to note Spiritual Markers left for you when you knew God had clearly guided you.

- Who in your young life poured into you? Think of someone in your life today who needs your mentoring now. We need not wait to be asked. Reach out to a young person and offer to come along side of them.

- What early events developed your "backbone for life"?

- Events and people contribute most to our character in preparing us for life after high school. Write a note of thanks to these people, or better yet, take them for lunch and tell them directly while you still can. (On a Reunion trip to Wisconsin several years later, I looked forward to seeing many of the people mentioned in this Stone. Fr. Leahy and Sr. Honoré had been called to glory. I was truly heartsick and saddened I hadn't thanked them earlier.)

- Share your memories of your high school years with your grandchildren. They will love knowing you were once young!

- Take as many of your photographs as you can, of when you were young, and help make a family tree for your children or grandchildren.

- Take your grandchildren on a Childhood Trip back to your hometown. Show them places you lived, went to school, worshipped, meeting relatives they've never met!

- As a grandparent, think of whom you might support for a mission trip or Christian camp experience.

And He said to me, "My grace is sufficient for you,
for My strength is made perfect in weakness."

— *2 Corinthians 12:9*

STONE 3   LIFE WITHOUT A COMPASS

I decided to take the Greyhound bus home from school for the start of semester break. With final exams a week away, I liked the idea of studying at home while spending time with my mom. But she had already made plans to spend the weekend with my grandmother, who lived about ninety miles away. She dropped me off at a friend's house on her way out of town. She looked forward to returning home on Sunday evening. A half hour later, she returned, saying, "I just had to come back! I forgot to tell you I love you!"

My mom did not come home Sunday evening. She called to say she felt ill and could not make the drive until morning. She was admitted to the hospital the next day. My older brother and I made a trip up to my grandmother's home in Sheboygan to see her. Once there, the doctors explained they could not make a diagnosis because she was too weak even to endure any tests.

With strict hospital visiting hours in those days, we left her at eight that evening, promising we'd both be back in the morning. As we quietly walked down the dark corridor to leave, the nurse came running after us, saying my mother wanted to say good-bye to us again. When I reached her bedside, she told me to come close. I bent down to her face and she softly whispered, "I love you, honey. Always be a good girl and ...stay ...as sweet ...as you are."

My brother and I drove home silently, both hoping our mother would improve by morning. I would be going to 6:30 Mass in the morning, but I told him to call me when he heard any news. The next morning the weatherman forecast blizzard-like wind and snow conditions, warning all cars to stay off the roads. Though I normally walked the six blocks to church, I obeyed the nudge to stay home.

At 6:30, my grandmother called with an urgency in her voice: "Get dressed, Joanne. Your brother is on his way and you must come quickly. Your mother has taken a turn for the worse. I don't think she'll make it. Drive safely and hurry!"

The drive that normally took an hour and a half took us four and a half hours. It was the worst blizzard the coast of Lake Michigan had seen in years. Every few miles, my brother and I had to get out of the car to scrape the windshield wipers off the frozen glass. There were no other cars on the road. Then the car heater stopped working. We were cold and scared. I prayed the whole way for my brother's old car not to stall or break down. The storm worsened with every mile we drove. I could feel the hand of God upon us, going before us as we crawled those last few miles. It was almost noon by the time we arrived.

We ran up to my mother's hospital room as quickly as our frozen feet could take us. Turning into her room, we found no one there—just an empty bed, stripped of linens. Having worked as a candy striper at our hospital the previous summer, I knew what that meant. A nurse told us my grandmother and family members were expecting us in the waiting area. Instead, I asked her how to get to the hospital chapel. All I wanted was to run into the arms of my Savior. I couldn't believe my mother was gone.

My mother Dorothy Emma

HIS FOOTSTEPS : MAJOR LOSS

Sometime later, my brother and grandmother came for me in the chapel. We drove to my grandmother's home in silence, my head swirling with thoughts. I was only nineteen years old, and I had lost my mother. I would never be able to ask her advice or have her listen to my problems or cry with me over a lost love. She would not be there to help me pick out my wedding dress or see me walk down the aisle or cry for joy with me on my wedding day. She would not be there when I had my babies, to hold them and kiss them and spoil them. My babies would grow up never knowing their grandmother.

We would miss all the special occasions and holidays of a lifetime. We would never celebrate another milestone together. I would never be able to take care of her when she grew old. My frozen body thawed to numbness.

Since my parents were divorced, my brother and I made our mother's funeral arrangements. My close group of friends from school in Madison drove to be with me for her memorial and graveside service. My father joined us, cried with us and sat with us as a family to say our good-byes. He hosted the dinner following the service and paid for hotel rooms for all my friends.

HIS TENDERNESS : ONE LAST TOUCH

The next night, having returned from the funeral I stayed alone at our cozy one-bedroom apartment. I sat in the window seat in the living room and remembered the many talks I'd had with my mother while sitting there. I would look out and share all the dreams I had for my life. She often told me how special that vision of me was to her—curled up on the cushion with the window wide open, the fresh air making sheer white Priscilla curtains stream in the wind. As I sat there that evening, I sensed

"*Time is the only comforter*

for the loss of a mother,

but missing her continues forever."

— *Jane Welsh Carlyle*

my mother's comforting voice. It may sound crazy to some, but whether it was grief or the Lord's care, I heard her tell me, "Honey, thank you for the most beautiful funeral. I am fine, and you will be, too. Don't worry about me. I love you."

I sat in that window seat well into the night.

The next morning my dad and brother came to help me pack up the apartment. Everything went to my brother's place, because he had the space. I stayed with my dad and his family while we worked things out, taking only my clothes with me. For the next few months, I slept on the pullout sofa in the dining room of a two-bedroom duplex with my dad, stepmom, and three half-sisters, ages six months and six and nine years old. We loved spending time together, but you can imagine how the arrangement stretched us all.

With the loss of my mom, I went from a primary member of my mother's household to a secondary member in my father's. In his eyes, I was always his daughter; but I now ranked below my stepmom and her family. I struggled with a profound loss of belonging. I could see the fragile line my dad was walking with my presence in their home. I was grateful and helped out in any way I could, especially when it involved playing with my sisters. I'd often wake up with all of them snuggled next to me in the small sofa bed.

REDIRECTED

I had missed all of my final exams at the University, requiring me to take "incompletes" in my classes. Furthermore, my dad told me he could not afford tuition and room and board expenses for me while supporting his wife and three young children. I could not return to school in Madison. I'd have to find a full-time job at home, but I could still take night classes at the University of Wisconsin extension in Milwaukee.

I returned to campus only to talk with my professors, clean out my room, and say good-bye to my dear roommate, Fern. I drove home for good with the same George Donovan who had been so generous in driving me up to Madison just six months earlier. He encouraged me to be steadfast in my commitment to be the first one in my family to graduate from college. He made me promise to finish school, no matter how long it took.

I cried all the way home. It was one of those days I will never forget in a lifetime. In one week I had lost my mother, my school, my friends, my home, and everything in it. What are you thinking as you read this now? I wish I could hear your story. Perhaps you have lost your mother; perhaps, like this, it's a story of loss that has knocked the very life and breath out of you—a spouse; a child. Perhaps you have yet to navigate this stone in your river. Life doesn't prepare you for it, but as I look back at that crossroad, I see that God did. He brought me close to Him the last two years of high school and those three weeks of my convent summer. I had spiritual seeds without deep roots, but I felt the love of Christ wash over me. He reminded me that He had a plan for my life.

And the Lord will guide you continually
and satisfy your desire in scorched places
and make your bones strong;
and you shall be like a watered garden,
like a spring of water, whose waters do not fail.

— Isaiah 58:11

HIS DELAYS : HOPE DEFERRED

Since I had also missed the cutoff date for spring enrollment, I took the semester off and applied for a full-time job at Bruce Publishing Company in downtown Milwaukee. For my interview, I was given three books to read and review—that night. I ended up with a wonderful position as the Assistant to the Editor, Mr. Bruce, Jr., a gruff, fast-paced workhorse with bushy eyebrows, unruly gray hair and a big stomach held back by red suspenders. Each day he would pass my desk, toss me a book and say, "Here, young lady, have the review on my desk by 8 o'clock in the morning!" He taught me a great deal about writing and editing and definitely toughened my skin to writing criticism. I loved typing my reviews on my old, black Remington typewriter, firmly hitting one key at a time, the old-fashioned way.

God showed Himself in the pain and loss of my mom, in quiet moments and long nights. One day, while reading a book for review, I happened upon a quote I loved so much, I typed it on a small index card and carried it with me in my wallet for years. It read:

> *"Remember, my petite, to be happy,*
> *for when you are unhappy, you grow sad,*
> *and when you are sad, you grow lonely,*
> *and when you are lonely, you grow bitter;*
> *and a sad, lonely, bitter woman has nothing,*
> *neither friends, love nor contentment."*
>
> — *Colette, French author*

MY FAMILY

God had guided me to an incredible job where I discovered my love of books and of writing. Yet despite this blessing, I struggled with feelings of being displaced and terribly alone. I didn't know what to do with my grief. The way ahead looked shrouded in uncertainty.

I was so envious of friends who still had their moms, whom they could go to for help and direction, someone to laugh with, trust, and confide in, knowing she loved you no matter what. I missed my mom every day.

I'd see friends of hers who would ask how I was; I would see my aunts and uncles and they'd ask how I was; but all I wanted to do was talk about my mother with friends and family who loved her and had watched her grow up. I wanted to hear stories I had never heard before—what she was like as a young girl, before she married and had my brother and me. She was only forty-six years old when she died. At nineteen, I was so busy sharing my life concerns with her that I didn't leave time or space to know her. I was breaking away from her "apron strings," trying to discover who I was on my own. I wasn't even sure if she knew the Lord. How could I never have talked with her about her faith? Oh, how I hope she is praying for me and waiting for me in Heaven! Today, if you are struggling with similar thoughts, I encourage you with His Word:

And in the same way the Spirit also helps us in our weakness,
for we do not know how to pray as we should,
but the Spirit Himself intercedes for us
with groanings too deep for words.

— Romans 8:26

Look back to a time when you felt alone and without direction, when you felt you were living your life without a compass. Examine how God was before you and beside you, even when you were not aware of Him, how He guided you and held you in the palm of His hand. What Spiritual Markers did He place in your life to show you the way?

SUMMER DAYS

The month of June finally came, bringing all of my college friends home from school. We were together as much as our summer jobs would permit, spending weekends at the lake and late afternoons at the beach, sharing memories of our early years together while exploring dreams for our future professions. Many summer evenings found us barbecuing with parents and eating famous Wisconsin sweet corn and brats.

That first year of school left us thinking we knew everything and yet knowing nothing. We were already experiencing profound love and loss. I spent many late-night chats with my next-door neighbor and "best guy friend," Tim. After everyone in our respective homes had gone to bed, Tim would throw small pebbles up to the dining room window where I was in bed reading my assignments for work. Tim lived his life carrying the heavy load of a family legacy of tragedy. We'd meet outside on the porch and share thoughts we couldn't share with other friends who hadn't experienced what we had lost.

Those small pebbles were strewn across both our rivers of life, and neither of us realized their importance. Yet God used those pebbles to provide a bond and Spiritual Marker in both of our lives, bringing us together to help each other navigate this stone of emptiness and grief.

My dear friend Tim

As the end of summer drew near, Tim told me he didn't want to return to school. I became upset with him, because he was a University of Wisconsin athlete and honor student. He succeeded in all areas; academic, athletic, and humanitarian. He lived his life with excellence. He had been voted "Most Likely to Succeed" in our

high school class, and I couldn't imagine him not going back. The last night of the summer, we all gathered together for our farewells. But Tim didn't show up.

I never saw him again. A few weeks into the semester, Tim drove to his family cabin on the lake, tied his two treasured Irish Setters to a tree and walked out into the water in the dark of night, leaving behind his mother, three sisters, teachers, coaches, friends, and two dogs who adored him.

One night soon after his loss, I gathered as many of those precious pebbles I could find at the base of my window and placed them in a small rectangle tin box under my pillow. Tim was the most humble, kind, loving, smart, fun, talented person in our young world. He was forever sealed in all of our hearts.

Dear Reader, almost everyone I've ever known has lost someone young who was very close. Gather your own pebbles from life and include them among your stones in the river.

THE BEAUTY OF A BUS RIDE

In September, I was enrolled in night classes at the University of Wisconsin-Milwaukee, while keeping my full-time position at the publishing company. I took the bus to school and work each day. When winter arrived, the snowplows piled the snow so high along the route the bus driver could barely see us to pick us up! The forty-minute ride, morning and evening, gave me a great chance to read every day.

I also loved people watching. Each man, woman and child boarding the bus each day had a story. All wearing their heavy winter coats, they would move to the back of the bus 'til they were squished like sardines; then upon reaching downtown, one after another, they would step off the bus and into their lives. I loved to imagine where they lived and what they did, wondering what their families were like. Thus, my bus-books and bus-stories were woven into my daily commute, sewing the threads of humanity into something lasting and beautiful.

As I wondered about their lives, I wondered when God was going to tell me what the next chapter of my life was going to hold. We live our life in chapters, don't we? Some are brief, some are long, some are endearing, and others we simply endure. A few have long-lasting effects, creating the very foundation of our life. The tears and years of my life in our small village of Shorewood had made me who I was. They would be part of me forever, but I began to sense that this chapter was coming to an end.

For the first time in my life, I felt discouragement and doubt taking hold of my heart and undermining my world. I struggled with the loss of my mom every day, compounded by being displaced in my small family world. I felt the rudder slipping on my sailboat. I was in unfamiliar waters with no compass to find my way home.

CALIFORNIA DREAMIN'

Over the same summer we lost Tim, my friend Judy had begged me to join her on a trip west. We both had relatives in California, so we tentatively planned our trip for the summer before our junior year. I broke the news to my Dad in April 1961.

Judy and I had done extensive research on where we could afford to live in California and finish school at a state university. We planned to spend a few weeks enjoying our relatives, after which we would find jobs and an apartment. We settled on five cities, each of which we wrote on a piece of paper and dropped into my dad's well-worn Milwaukee Braves baseball cap. Excited and confident, we ran into the living room and asked my dad to "seal the deal." Not impressed with our bravado, my dad reached down into his cap and drew out a piece of paper and slowly opened it, announcing, "Long Beach, California!"

What were we thinking? He thought we were crazy, confident we wouldn't last six months. We were sane enough to realize he could be right—but we were going to take the adventure anyway.

HIS SILENCE : TRIALS AND TESTING

My first year in California was a disaster. Judy and I enrolled in night classes at a junior college until we could gain California residency for in-state tuition. Being without a car in California made life challenging. I left at 6:30 in the morning by bus to arrive at work by 8 o'clock, work until 5 o'clock, and then catch a bus to school for classes from 6 o'clock to 9 o'clock in the evening and another bus to be home by 10 o'clock! My bus books and people watching were replaced by studying every minute I could.

Surprisingly to us, money didn't go very far, so we lived on peanut butter and toast. We were grateful for our aunts and uncles who took pity on us. The older couple who managed our apartment complex invited us to join them whenever we passed their barbecue. When Christmas came, neither of us had money to make the trip home. I spent the holiday with my aunt and uncle, for which I was quite grateful. But I was far from home—and very homesick.

Judy had met a great guy almost immediately and spent most of her time with him. Soon she announced she was moving to San Francisco to live with his family until they married. My dad suggested I move in with my distant cousin and her roommates who lived close to my school until I could graduate and return home. They were older with full-time jobs and lots of friends, so studying became impossible.

THE HOUND OF HEAVEN

I certainly did not make a conscious decision to move away from the Lord, but at some point, I realized I had moved far away from my spiritual life. I no longer went to church, because I was so tired on the weekends. I had no car or friends to attend with me. Looking back, I didn't even have any believing friends, and it didn't even occur to me to notice. I was spiritually adrift—and spiritual drifting colors all of our choices. I realized I had lost my way, the way of God's Truth, my True North. I was truly living life without a compass.

As I wrote this Stone, I met a young woman from Paris who had been traveling for two years to learn English and learn about the world. She was in her final few months of touring the United States, doing short stays with families here and there while working for her keep. Her family wanted her to come home and even told her she was being selfish to pursue these dreams. She was trying to find out who she was, so she could be a whole person when she settled down to marry and raise a family. She had always said that age twenty-eight was her limit to be married, and here she was—twenty-eight and still looking. She would love a great guy but she feared they were all taken!

After listening to her story, I simply looked at her and smiled. "You're searching, and God's calling," I said. "He is the Hound of Heaven, and He will chase you down the labyrinthine halls to bring you home to Him. We have a hole in our heart that can only be filled by Him." She began to softly cry as the Holy Spirit touched her that night. After several minutes, she confessed, "Yes, I think it's time to go home. It's time to stop wandering. And I will pray and ask God to give me faith."

Have you ever found yourself without a compass to find your True North, feeling life was sweeping you along on a path you couldn't leave, one you hadn't even chosen? What led to your wanderings? Was it loss, loneliness, isolation, pain, disappointment, hurt? Was it discontent, discouragement, a longing for adventure, or searching for you know not what?

Even in my own spiritual drifting, God didn't change. I was in a desert like Hagar, watched by the same God –

El Roi, The God-Who-Sees-Me.

— *Genesis 16:13*

There are no circumstances in our lives that escape His fatherly awareness and care. God knows us and our troubles.

We can be hard on ourselves during life's changes and transitions, this "coming of age" when we so painfully grow into adults. In taking responsibility for ourselves, we examine, identify, and sort out who we will be. Sometimes we choose the wrong path and suffer a long detour before finding our True North again. Some believe God has abandoned them because they feel alone and lost. The longer we drift, the greater the consequences.

My sisters and me

- We never know when we will have said the last "I love you" to our mom or dad. Say it often and celebrate their presence in your life.

- Listen to the still small voice in your heart. Heed the "Stops" and the "Go's". God knows what awaits us. He goes before us.

- Think of the companions who God provided for you in your loss, the angels in the form of friends He sent. Perhaps you could be an angel to a friend who's grieving the loss of someone they love. Call them, take meals to them, sit with them, and listen. Just being with them tells them you care. Include them with your family for meals and outings.

- The intensity of our grief is the intensity of our love for one we have lost. Be kind, gentle, and forgiving to those who don't understand. Those who have also suffered loss will understand.

- Experiences of spiritual drifting are often the result of pain, loss, disappointment, self-doubt, and pride. God sees you and will never let you go. Hear Him calling.

- Have you ever felt lost and without a compass? Spend quiet time with God every day. Be still and listen. God promises if we seek him, we will find him. Pray for Faith. Pray for God to show you how to pray. He will not disappoint.

- Do not be discouraged—it means you are without courage. Be strong and courageous! Stand guard at the entrance to your mind. Disregard the lies the enemy puts in your thoughts! He is real and "he comes only to steal and kill, and destroy!" (John 10:10). You can never be without courage when God is by your side. Feel Him pour it into your heart.

- Don't sit on the outskirts of your Christian circle where you are prey to be "picked off" by the enemy. We are meant to live our lives in community. The embers of our hearts are "stoked" by fellowship with other believers. Find a small group you can be involved with from church or volunteer where you can serve.

- Often times we have to hit bottom before we realize how far we have strayed. The longer we drift, the greater the consequences.

He will be like a tree firmly planted by a stream of water,
which yields its fruit in its season; And its leaf does not wither:
And in whatever he does, he prospers.

— Psalm 1:3

STONE 4   MARRIAGE

I knew that finishing my education was the only way I could fulfill both my dream of teaching and my promise to George. I was desperate for that first year to end so I could begin my last two years of work at Cal State University at Long Beach. Then I would be back on track.

I met with the Dean of Admissions to plan my course study, and afterwards ran into Jean, the daughter of the Dean, waiting for her dad to go to lunch. We became friends the moment we met. She was also enrolled in the Education Department, working at school between classes. She invited me to meet her friends for dinner that evening. I know that God orchestrated that meeting. I will forever give Him praise and glory, because it changed the trajectory of my life.

Within weeks, I had settled into a darling apartment with Jean and three new friends, all teaching majors, and enrolled in classes with a part-time job in the Dean of Admissions Office. God is so good!

My new group of friends had been at Cal State Long Beach for two years already, so sorority and fraternity groups enlarged my world, as well. Between Jean, Mary, Linda, Mary Jo, and Martha—not to mention school, work, and study— my life was full, busy, and fun. One memorable day, a girl from Minnesota came to my New Student Admissions window. Bonnie and I discovered we shared a few classes together. Being from the Midwest state of Wisconsin myself, we laughed over not missing the frigid winters back home. Bonnie also missed her family. My family had just spent a month in California, so their absence was freshly painful. We both wondered if we had made the right decision by moving so far away.

I contemplated returning home after graduation. Then one morning in October of 1963, my dad phoned early in the morning to invite me to lunch. I had to ask him to repeat himself. Lunch? "Dad, I'm in California and you're in Wisconsin! What do you mean?"

"Well, Sweetie, I have some good news for you. Rose and I and the girls are moving to California, and we want to find a home where we can all live together again. I'm flying out there today. We'll discuss it over lunch." A father's love knows no bounds.

My dad did not waste any time moving his family and business to California. He couldn't wait to sell his shovels and snowplows in exchange for shorts and a backyard barbecue. I said goodbye to my roommates and moved into our new family home in Long Beach. My stepmother never forgave my father for their move from her family in Wisconsin and I soon found myself, at the age of twenty-two, sharing a bedroom with my thirteen-year-old sister who had an eight o'clock bedtime. My best time for study came at the dining room table between eleven in the evening and two or three in the morning when the house was quiet.

My stepmother cried from Thanksgiving to Christmas, missing the traditions of holiday preparations with her mother and sister, depressed by the warm sunny days replacing her Wisconsin dreams of a white Christmas. It took me some time to adjust to the idea of losing my hometown of Shorewood for Long Beach, but of one thing I was sure—I was thrilled to have us all together again as my only family.

MY MARRIAGE STRUGGLE

Dear Reader, this Stone of marriage is difficult for me to share. From the time I was young, I vowed to my mom, dad, and close friends that I would never, never, never get divorced. Three generations before me had been divorced, and I was determined to break the cycle. I knew firsthand the pain that divorce caused for my brother and me, as well as for my parents, family, and friends. I struggled with a sense of belonging. I was always aware of my poor self-esteem, comparing myself to those who came from intact families. I always came up short, never good enough in my eyes, but keeping these thoughts and doubts to myself. I loved people and always strove to look good on the outside, while feeling insecure on the inside. Perhaps that's how we all feel.

The loss of my mom continued to weigh heavily on my mind as I struggled to achieve a true sense of maturity and a strong compass to guide me forward. I was unprepared and ill equipped for navigating this stone in my river of life called marriage. When our perspective on life is still being developed, we're more susceptible to making mistakes. In such a stage of life, it's easy to align ourselves with those who agree with us instead of those with wisdom to guide us well.

If any of you lacks wisdom, let him ask of God, who gives to all men
generously and without reproach, and it will be given to him.
But let him ask in faith without any doubting,
for the one who doubts is like the surf of the sea
driven and tossed by the wind.

—James 1:5-6

To further complicate things, there was also a movement afloat across the nation called the Women's Liberation Movement. The aim was to "liberate" women from the ties of the "unfulfilling role of being a wife," encouraging them to enter the work force, earn an income, and stand on their own without men. The headlines took over the evening news as well as college and cafeteria conversations on every college campus across the country.

The consequences were, in my humble opinion, devastating to our nation. Divorce rates skyrocketed. Families were torn apart. Sitting in a secular college classroom every day, I heard what a just movement it was and how the breakdown of the family unit was necessary for women to be free. We were told women should expect to have it all. In truth, the movement served as a catalyst for moral relativism.

MY MARRIAGE STORY

My college friend, Bonnie, and her husband wanted me to meet a friend who had recently returned from spending two years in Germany in the army. Their friend had already graduated from college where he had been in a fraternity. He now shared a house in Long Beach with four of them and already had a good sales position with an international company. They introduced me to Chuck on a blind date.

He was fun and handsome! He was also a gentleman. He picked me up at my house and came in to meet my parents and sisters. He easily made conversation with everyone. Before long, we were dating steadily. We spent most of our time with large groups of his fraternity friends and their girlfriends. We had a party for every reason and every season. We were carefree and enjoying life even while working hard in school and our careers. One by one, our friends got engaged, set up house, and started new families.

Eleven months later, we were married. Although divorced from his mother, Chuck's father pastored a small church in the South. We asked him to marry us in my home church, along with my own pastor whom I wanted to officiate. We attended six Preparation for Marriage classes with my pastor. Because Chuck was a non-Catholic,

Chuck and me,
Jamaica 1969

he agreed to raise our children in the Catholic Church.

We had a beautiful church wedding with Jean, my sisters, and my brother and Chuck's friends in the wedding party. My Dad proudly walked me down the aisle, quietly singing "Here Comes the Bride" with tears in his eyes. I cried with him and clung to him, not wanting to let go and missing my mother so much it hurt.

Chuck and I threw ourselves into our marriage. I kept my promise to George and graduated from college after seven long years. He and Betty even sent us a gift to put in the bank toward our first house. I eagerly prepared for my student teaching assignment to complete the fifth year for my teaching credential. First graders were awaiting me in September!

Just into summer, Chuck and I were surprised and delighted to learn we were expecting our first baby! I was several weeks along, and calculating the dates, figured I could almost make it to the end of the teaching year. We decided not to tell anyone but our families until we were further along in weeks. I loved my fun, lovable, spontaneous, and energetic first-graders and made it my mission to teach them all to read by the time they graduated first grade.

Parents Open House Night was held the third week of school. I spent days preparing our classroom, proudly displaying the children's art and science projects, arranging the reading circle with their Phonics books on their chairs, while brightly-decorated bulletin boards proclaimed the alphabet in all its artistic and academic importance. The children were so excited for me to meet their parents. They made freshly-decorated nametags for each of them. I so loved teaching.

As I drove home to change clothes for my big event, the cramping abruptly began. It was soon followed by other indications that I was in the process of having a miscarriage. I called my principal, who comforted me and assured me he would take

SHANNON, MY LOVE FULFILLED

over my classroom that evening. Coming home from the hospital without a baby in my arms was a loss I simply couldn't express. I cried for days. My dear, precious mother-in-law, Neva, came to be with me every day. We cried together.

My sweet little first graders brought me happiness every day of that school year. I was so sad to have them leave in June. They had all become my little babies throughout the year. I taught Marine Biology for fifth grade summer school and saved all my paychecks from that first year for our first house. In 1968, we put $6,000 down toward a $29,000 three-bedroom home! The next October, we were pregnant again!

I went into labor a hot night that next July while knitting my baby's blanket and watching Neil Armstrong take the first walk on the moon. Shannon O'Brien was born July 22, 1969. The headlines in the newspaper read: "Small Step for Man, Giant Leap for Mankind." But as far as we were concerned, all the Heaven's had opened.

We were a family. In spite of all the Women's Lib propaganda, I was thrilled to be able to stay home with my beautiful baby daughter and be a mommy to her. It was an answer to all my prayers. Our families were loving and supportive. We spent many evenings with my dad and Rose and girls, eager for them to share hugs and kisses with their granddaughter and niece. Several of our friends were also having babies, so the weekends found us together for picnics and potluck dinners. We joined my family on Sundays for my Dad's famous barbecue feasts.

The next year I was pregnant again—and miscarried three months later. The doctor suggested we wait at least a year to try again. The waiting was unbearable as I had dreams of having four or five children. We were so happy when, after just five months, we told our families we were expecting again. Five months later, I miscarried again. That Christmas, I hung three silver bells on our tree, each engraved with a name — John, Michael, and David, my precious Angels in Heaven.

HIS SOVEREIGNTY : LOSS OF A CHILD

There is one loss that is impossible to imagine, let alone experience: losing your child. When you lose a spouse, you are a widow. When you lose a parent, you are an orphan. But when you lose your precious child, there is no name for it—it is unspeakable. Unfortunately, we don't often speak of it for fear of not knowing what to say! The pain to those who carried the child and loved him or her is unfathomable and will live with the survivors forever. I don't know how people survive such a tragedy without the faith and hope of Christ.

Thank God for His gift of faith, for without it we would all be lost. When faced with tragedy, there will be questions we can't answer this side of eternity. But God is faithful! There will be gifts of God's goodness to help carry the burden of your loss. Those who love you will hurt, heal, and hope with you. Remember our Heavenly Father knows how it feels to lose a child. You are not alone on the journey. Mary witnessed her Son's painful death on the cross. If you have suffered the loss of a child, know that God knows your pain. He loves you unconditionally, and He is sovereign.

After my miscarriages, I tried to move on. I went back to teaching and kept my mind occupied and distracted. The first miscarriage was the most difficult because I came home empty-handed. All my dreams were in a bundle of sadness and loss, laying on the to-be nursery room floor.

Knowing what I know now, if I could have written my younger self a note and slipped it in my Teachers Lesson Planner Book at the time of my loss, this is the note I would have written:

Dear Heart,

Such a big tidal wave of grief sweeping over you today. I am so sorry. I know how much you wanted this baby to hold in your arms, snuggle, and love, how much you wanted to be a family.

Give yourself time to taste the tears as you sit in the rocking chair meant for two. Take all the time you need to grieve and heal. The anguish, sadness, and disbelief will live with you for some time, along with the emptiness of not having your baby inside of you and feeling those little flutters of life.

Some emotions will have no name. It will be hard to express yourself in ways that make sense, but try. Allow other women who have experienced loss in their miscarriages to share their sorrow with you as you share yours. Rest and heal, in body and soul. Understand how others want to comfort and love you. Trust that you will be a mother again. Dedicate your baby back to the Lord for safe keeping until you meet again in Heaven.

Your due date will be hard. Baby showers and baby births of your friends will be hard. Be kind to yourself when you think no one understands. Be forgiving of others who say insensitive things or don't know what to say to give you comfort.

You will feel at a loss for some time, but you are strong. Trust the Lord to be your anchor. Simply because family or friends don't talk about your loss doesn't mean they don't care. You're not alone. God is sovereign. Rest in His Hands. He works all things together for good.

By then, anxieties were running high, as the last two miscarriages had taken a severe emotional toll on our marriage. I was heartbroken and fearful of not being able to carry another pregnancy to term. I longed for my husband's attention and words of encouragement. He didn't know what to do with me. Our marriage was in trouble. We had struggled with our relationship from the beginning, but neither of us could discuss it with the other. In addition, things had begun to surface that I could not live with for a lifetime. As the reality of our incompatibility set in, the silence began between us, a relational wasteland with no highs and no lows, though we were careful to cover it up in front of others.

My ultimatum to Chuck was strong: "Either we go for counseling or I can't go on." After we began marriage counseling, things went well for several months. Even though our relationship was struggling, we both wanted to try to get pregnant again, because Shannon needed a little sister or brother! As the new year began, I was thrilled to find I was pregnant again! We agreed to continue counseling and make our marriage work. We hoped the three miscarriages were responsible for the chasm between us. We also hoped all would be solved with the arrival of another baby. Each day was like walking on eggshells, trying so hard not to do anything that would precipitate a miscarriage. Family and friends encouraged us and helped us prepare our new baby's room.

Meghan O'Brien was born October 5, 1973. Once again, all the Heavens opened and blessed us with another precious daughter. We loved to tell people the only thing better than one daughter was two daughters!

That holiday season brought such happiness to our families and to us. I even dared to think we could keep our marriage together and have more children. But after the Christmas season, I discovered that nothing was ever going to change.

Shannon and Meghan— loving sisters

MEGHAN, MY PUREST JOY

At the counselor's suggestion, Chuck and I agreed to a trial separation. My dad asked me to give it another try. I had never disobeyed my father. I would do anything he asked of me. Chuck and I continued counseling with intermittent dating for another year.

The days of rebellion begin in disobedience, often from being denied what we want or feel we need. I did have great needs in this relationship. It must have been my fault. I wasn't good enough, not lovable enough, not _____ enough. The truth is I had tried to fix my marriage without God being in the picture at all. All the architectural plans, wood, hammers, nails, levelers, tape measures, or cement could not keep our marriage together. We were missing the only One who could quench our thirst with streams of Living Water to minister to our hurting souls.

All marriages are touched by disease in some manner or degree. Because we are human, we are sinners and our sin creates moral bacteria that can spread. There may be a sickness of the body or of the mind. There may be unfaithfulness to a spouse, to the family, and to God. There may be pride, selfishness, and narcissism that eat away at the little daily stones of the way. There may be abuse—physical, verbal, or emotional. There may be dependencies, alcoholism, and other addictions that impede emotional availability as it draws the very life and breath out of both partners.

Divorce is a real fact of life. Often God allows us to make mistakes, just as we allow our children to make mistakes. We are God's children, even when we turn our back on Him and refuse to obey. Chuck and I intended to keep the vows we had made to each other on our wedding day. We had two beautiful daughters who became the most important consideration of love in our lives. We truly cared for one another, even through the broken commitment of our wedding vows.

Even as we separated, we promised we would never say an unkind word to our daughters about the other or to other people. We promised we would never use our

daughters to get back at or punish each other. Knowing the love of a daughter for her father, we chose to respect and honor one another for the sake of our two precious daughters. Our greatest gifts from our marriage were our perfect children. Our greatest job was to protect them from as much pain as possible by showing care and consideration for each other while showering our children with all the love in our hearts.

God allows us to make mistakes so we can learn from our mistakes. If there were any lessons in this painful decision, we promised each other we would find them. Perhaps one of the lessons of divorce is to treasure and take care of our marriage. Both husband and wife will be navigating their own respective stones in the river. Each person in the marriage relationship has a choice on how to manage each stone as it is revealed to him or her. To have such an intimate relationship of the marriage covenant between two people exposed to judgment by others heightens the level of pain they're each experiencing. The most loving thing we can do is to respect their marriage boundaries without any weight or advice. Take it to the Lord in prayer.

The most life-changing stone in a woman's life may well be her divorce stone. Is there a right way and a wrong way? I believe there's an important lesson here, that each the mother and father strive to navigate it with as much intentional integrity and respect for the sake of their children as possible. We can either go through it by tearing someone down in order to raise ourselves up, or we can choose to move forward with all carefulness and humility. Winning isn't the goal. The goal is protecting our children for the glory of God. While we're at it, we need to let go of the all hurt, anger, and sadness bleeding from our hearts, and the only way to unleash the burden is to forgive.

I will never be able to justify our divorce in God's eyes. I can only attempt to explain why it occurred.

HIS TEACHING : THE VOWS WE MAKE

In a Christian marriage, we exchange traditional wedding vows to one another. "I, _____, take thee _____, to be my wedded _____, to have and to hold, from this day forward, for better, for worse, for richer, for poorer, in sickness and in health, to love and to cherish, for as long as we both shall live."

We acknowledge Christ as the Cornerstone of our marriage, the foundational stone on which the Marriage Stone is built.

In architectural terms, Christ is also the Keystone of a marriage. This Keystone is the central stone at the summit of an arch, locking the whole of the arch together. The Keystone is the Stone upon which everything else depends. It is the stone that takes all the stress of the structure upon itself, meaning Christ takes all the stress of our marriage upon Himself when we offer up and surrender our marriages to Him.

How can you build a strong marriage to withstand the winds of time without the Cornerstone and Keystone of your marriage being Christ? Suppose you and your spouse plan to build your forever house on your chosen location. Your builder will ask you several questions: Do you have architectural plans? Have you thought about your foundation? What materials will support the foundation? How much time and care are you prepared to invest to build a house that will last for a lifetime? Are you committed to invest whatever it takes?

All those same questions apply to building a strong marriage. Ask them early and don't rest until you get answers you both agree on. Marriage is sacred. And it is critical that you both share the same understanding of God's role in your marriage. Being equally yoked, as the Bible puts it when two Christians marry, makes the marriage stronger. The plow moves together and more efficiently and smoothly when both are in agreement. When you both share a love for God, no one and nothing can separate you. He alone can bring health, healing, and redemption, although sometimes it comes later, after the marriage has ended.

One of the greatest privileges for parents and grandparents is that of praying for our children and grandchildren's spouses. I thank God that He hears my prayers for my grandchildren, most of whom are presently unmarried.

Pray for your spouse always, even before you marry. One good exercise when you are praying for your spouse-to-be is to sit down with pen and paper and think of all the qualities you would most like to have in a spouse. Write down everything that's important to you. Keep it in a safe place. When you meet a guy you think is special, take out your list and see how he measures up. If he doesn't, don't waste your time dating him! And while you're at it, make another list of the qualities to develop in yourself to attract the spouse of your dreams!

"This Is Our Love Story" is the title of your early days with your spouse, how you met, what your courtship was like, what attracted you to each other, and more. It is the story you will share over and over again in your lifetime with your children and friends. Your children will especially love to hear your love story over and over again. Make it wonderful!

HIS FORGIVENESS : WHAT'S LEFT AFTER THE STORM?

Divorce leaves a trail of heartbreak and broken dreams. The lifelong consequences cannot be measured. What do you do when Plan A doesn't work out? What do you do when you find yourself in Plan B? Who do you become? Which

Trust in the Lord with all your heart,

And do not lean on your own understanding.

In all your ways acknowledge Him

And He will make your paths straight.

— **Proverbs 3:5-6**

direction do you go after divorce splits your future path? Both parties feel like failures, but one thing is sure:

God is in every plan.

Do you wonder what God is doing in your life right now? We may think we know His will for our lives, yet we fail miserably. Whatever the circumstances, God can use it for our good and His glory. When we make mistakes, we learn to trust and respect the authority of God and to understand disobedience and its consequences. He uses our failures to grow our faith through confession and repentance. When was the last time God placed you in the "Penalty Box" to take you aside, to be silent and hear His voice, to prepare your pruning for major growth?

I was working on my pride, resentment, guilt, and shame. I was humbled to my lowest point. There was important "heart work" that needed to be done in my life, to learn of Him, to grow in wisdom and knowledge of Him and His plan for my life and that of my children.

I continued with marriage counseling. I needed to grieve the loss of my marriage and the dreams of having a house full of children. I needed to look at my part in the breakdown of this relationship, so I would not repeat my mistakes.

HIS RESTORATION : FINDING MY WAY AGAIN

I felt I had lost my way. I had also lost my spiritual footing. I was a mess. While I continued going to church with my girls, I no longer prayed nor sought God's will in any part of my life. And then I remembered my Dad's words again. "Pull up your bootstraps, sweetie! You can do it!"

I began with a Woman's Retreat, after which I spent time, along with my girls, in a prayer cocoon, so to speak, until I could find my True North again. I needed to know God still loved me. He gave me what only he could give—a new heart.

How do you rebuild your life after failure? How do rebuild your character? Your self-respect? Your sense of a "better" self? Your self-esteem? What about your precious children? Your parents and your family? How would you build a home filled with love when you have been disobedient and rebellious? You turn to the Lord and begin again.

Having had a teaching credential, I took a six-month course to acquire my certification to teach Lamaze Prepared Childbirth classes. I taught evening classes to expectant parents three nights a week at the hospital. After they had delivered their babies, the young moms and their newborns came to my house three mornings a week for New Mothering classes on breastfeeding, bathing, sleeping through the night, and general parenting help. Along with other young moms in the same exhausting boat, they brought their other young children with them. I had created a little pre-school environment for them and my own girls in the corner of the room. We had fun together as slowly, a new future began to emerge.

Along with my Lamaze students, several physicians sat in on my classes at the hospital, making sure I was teaching accurate medical information. The OB-GYN doctors also volunteered their time to give encouragement to the dads-to-be so they wouldn't faint in the delivery room! One of those doctors ended up becoming my second husband and stepfather to my girls.

Don King and I dated almost two years, giving all of us time to intentionally choose a new, positive direction that focused on the girls and a new commitment to God and marriage. Don already had a daughter, Kathy, married with two young children and a son in college, Earl. All of us needed time, so we took it slow.

When Don finally asked me to marry him, I called Chuck first. Because we had maintained a truly caring relationship, I wanted him to hear of our intentions from me. I wanted to reassure him that, as the girl's father, he would always be involved in

NEW TRADITIONS

their lives. I told him it would mean everything if he would give me his blessing to marry Don King. He gave it.

BEGINNING ANEW

We took baby steps into our future. Remarriage is an awesome challenge, one that takes incredible grit, strength, commitment, and faith. After seeking and receiving God's forgiveness for the failure of my marriage to Chuck, I experienced a new understanding of God's incredible grace. I sought Christian mentors to help me understand God's plan for marriage and committed myself wholeheartedly to pursuing His plan, considering my vows of marriage binding before the Lord.

He has not dealt with us according to our sins,
Nor rewarded us according to our iniquities.
For as high as the heavens are above the earth,
So great is His lovingkindness toward those who fear Him.
As far as the east is from the west,
So far has He removed our transgressions from us.

— Psalm 103:10-12

Before long, we found a new home, became a new family, and began to create a life together. Don was devoted to the girls and to me. For the first time since my mom had passed away, I was content and eager to devote all my time and attention into making a new home for all of us. Kathy and Earl were part of our family gatherings as their desires and time permitted.

Two years later we moved into a beautiful home overlooking the ocean. With Don

Sabot sailing, Alamitos Bay, Naples

being an avid sailor, our family joined the Yacht Club just down the Bayfront, which created an instant group of friends. We forged friendships for a lifetime with Fred and Sally, Ruth and Barry, Joanne and Jerry, their sons, daughters, and all our families. They became our forever friends.

Before long, the girls were active in swim team and sabot sailing lessons, lunches at the snack shop and afternoons playing in the pool while we moms visited, laughed, and exchanged good books and recipes. We took frequent sailing trips to Catalina, spending overnights on the boat, sharing food and fun with friends as they sailed over in tandem with us.

The summers flew by. Fall and winter were filled with school, ballet and dance lessons, seasonal sports, and ski trips! We skied in Snow Mass, Colorado for Christmas vacation, Palm Desert for Easter vacation, and Hawaii the first two weeks of summer vacation. We were making memories and giving the girls family traditions, while affording much needed time away for Don, a very busy OB-GYN with a large practice.

Don was the best stepfather in the world to Shannon and Meghan. He was loving, kind, fun, and very engaged in their lives. He always wanted what was best for them. We ate dinners together every night, with weekends for family time. Sundays, the girls spent the day with their dad and stepmom. Sounds perfect, I know. But let me tell you, the grass is never greener on the other side! The grass is greener where it is fed and watered!

> *"To love and to cherish, for better, for worse,*
> *for richer, for poorer, in sickness and in health,*
> *as long as we both shall live."*

Those six little adjectives describe the climate on any given day in all marriages. They encompass the ebb and flow of each of our unique marriages, made up of all the little pebbles in our river of life, rubbing together in the swift and tumultuous current of the water, ever shaping and molding us.

A longtime friend of mine recently lost her husband of forty-six years, both having been friends of mine. At Larry's Memorial, Joy wanted to say a word of thanks for all who had taken the time to come and share the love and memories we had with this great man.

"For me, no human being has ever loved me like he loved me. He always had my back, and when I was upset, he always told me things would turn out OK. But believe me, we weren't perfect and our marriage wasn't perfect. There were some days we really disliked each other and didn't want to stay married another day. We had times we wanted to leave, but never at the same time. So, if I wanted to leave, he would always talk me out of it, and if he had had it with me, I would tell him to wait, I'll do better.

For the last twenty of our forty-six years we never argued because we knew how it would turn out in the end anyway! We had learned to 'just let it pass...'

People would say, 'You and Larry have such a perfect marriage.' I would give them my funny look and say, 'You know, that's not true! What we DO have is RESPECT for each other, even though some days we hate each other!' Larry and I were never ugly with each other; he had my heart and I had his. And all of you who knew us know how much we loved each other with all our hearts."

We learn to love through it all—the good times, the hard times, times of plenty and good health and not. When rough waters come our way, we need to adjust our sails into the wind.

FOUR SEASONS OF MARRIAGE

In many ways, marriages unfold as if through different seasons. In the spring, we experience passion, exuberance, future dreams, house plans, family plans, early couple friendships, church fellowship, and a season of energy and enthusiasm so needed when adding children and starting and building careers.

Summer comes as we settle in to marriage, children, school, sports, activities, family friendships, building careers, work opportunities, family travel, missions, church fellowship, Bible studies, volunteering, leadership serving, entertaining friends, and family gatherings—whew! A busy, demanding season indeed.

Then fall arrives as children enter college and marriage, sports, working harder than ever, keeping up with increased financial demands, packing as much into a day as we can while we have our children at home, while making time for each other, travel, dreams and goals for retirement, entertaining, family gatherings, plus additional hours for a working mom to squeeze into her day. No wonder we feel tired.

Winter brings the joys of grandparenting! Travel, volunteering, hobbies, sports, friends and family gatherings, and enjoying the fruits of our labor—children, marriage, and career. We focus on turning successful lives into lives of significance for the Kingdom, stepping aside for others, passing the baton of holiday and family events, and working in the background, while still being present and engaged. This season often includes caregiving and health challenges that both test and demonstrate our love for one another.

Because marriage is a living, breathing, loving relationship between two people, change is a constant and inevitable part of life. Because marriage is such an important stone in the river of God's faithfulness, let us cherish this stone and commit to always enjoying it in all its shimmering, effervescent vibrancy even as life's swiftly flowing currents rage around us.

GRACE NOTES | *Marriage*

- When we follow the world's perspective, marriage leaves us hungry and thirsty, expecting our spouse to be and to provide everything for us. When we spend time with God in quietness and prayer, He will reveal His perspective for your life, filling your heart with peace, calm, and quiet. Seek His will for your life and your relationships. There is a clarity and insight that only comes from spending time with God. Ask for wisdom and understanding.

- I tell you truthfully and strongly as my Daddy did to me, "A family that prays together stays together." It will ensure your marriage and your legacy.

- Take the "D" word—divorce—off the table and never let it find its way back!

- Loss and crisis will come to your marriage. I pray you plant yourself on your knees and sometimes prostrate before God. Take your bleeding hearts before His Throne of Grace. Cling to Him. He is faithful. He is sovereign.

- Be a forgiver and a forgetter! Seek forgiveness from your spouse as soon as you feel the Holy Spirit's tap on your shoulder! "I'm sorry" should always paired with "Will you forgive me?"

- The secret of a long married life is to stick it out through the tough times! My "Covenant Sisters" have a favorite saying from the movie Frozen: "Let it go!"

- The grass is greener where it is fed and watered.

- As husbands and wives, we are the image bearers of God. The enemy would love nothing more than to destroy our marriage, our family, and our spiritual legacy for future generations. Keep up your guard!

- A good marriage is a triangle, with Christ at the top and with you and your spouse on the line below, each with head and heart looking up.

- As Gary Thomas asks in his book *Sacred Marriage*, "What if God designed marriage to make us holy more than to make us happy?"

Strength and dignity are her clothing,
*   and she laughs at the time to come.*
She opens her mouth with wisdom,
*   and the teaching of kindness is on her tongue.*
She looks well to the ways of her household,
*   and does not eat the bread of idleness.*

— **Proverbs 31:25–27**

STONE 5   MOTHERHOOD

I wish all the mothers I know and love could sit around my table and share their experiences with the challenges and joys of motherhood. I would ask, "Where were you when you first found out you were pregnant? What thoughts went through your mind? What dreams did you have for your baby boy or girl? How did you visualize your first years of being a mommy?" All my friends would fight to speak first as we shared the laughter and tears of our remarkable motherhood journeys.

Now on the other side of exhaustion, it's easy to smile at the early years when we quietly tiptoed into their nursery five times a night to glance upon their angelic face, snuggled with them in our bed each morning, savoring each fleeting, precious moment with this miracle from God. The first words, first steps, their beautiful smiles, and their sweet little bodies wiggling with excitement when we talked to them.

Toddler days meant sunny trips to the park, raisins and Cheerio snacks galore, mommy-and-me swim classes, and plenty of naps, trips to the pediatrician, birthday parties, and mounds of laundry. Then came preschool days with play dates, lunches of grilled cheese and chicken noodle soup, making Shrinky-Dinks, baking cookies in the oven, enjoying birthday parties at the playground, and time passing all too quickly. Before long, we were spending hours each week carpooling to soccer practice and dance lessons, finding last minute items for school projects due the next day, chaperoning field trips, and earning countless Girl Scout badges. Birthday parties were now held

in fun, loud places and the mounds of laundry lasted long into the night. All too quickly, high school years flew by with sports, driving lessons, SAT classes, lots of friends, and family dinners. We marked each occasion with a passionate silent prayer to savor each and every moment before our children took off on their next journey.

Looking back, the stages of raising our children seem a blur of chaos seasoned with feelings of stress and exhaustion. Especially when they are young, our lives are consumed with the needs of our children. At the same time, we juggle housekeeping and homemaking, friendships, and changing roles in our marriage. Yet despite the stress and challenges, we would never trade being a mother for a tranquil life. As each stage ends, it quickly becomes "the best" treasured memory.

HIS GIFT : THE CALL TO MOTHERHOOD

God has created us women to be nurturers by nature. In spite of what the Women's Lib movement tried telling me, motherhood is a high and holy calling. Our children are gifts from God to care for and prepare for a life and eternity with Him. The basic duty of motherhood and womanhood is to entrust to the next generation the message of God's faithfulness, whether through rearing our own children or spiritually nurturing others beyond the family circle.

Motherhood was the sweet spot of my life. Those years devoted to raising my two daughters, Shannon and Meghan, brought significance, purpose, and clarity to my life. It enlarged my heart in ways I never imagined possible. Those Holly Homemaker days were the best and busiest days of my life. Don and I loved it all—school activities, sports, home life, friendships, marriage, entertaining, and even the mounds of laundry!

Blessed is she who believed
that the Lord would fulfill
His promises to her.

— Luke 1:45

DAYS IN THE SUN

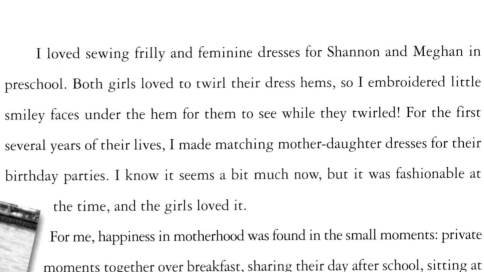

I loved sewing frilly and feminine dresses for Shannon and Meghan in preschool. Both girls loved to twirl their dress hems, so I embroidered little smiley faces under the hem for them to see while they twirled! For the first several years of their lives, I made matching mother-daughter dresses for their birthday parties. I know it seems a bit much now, but it was fashionable at the time, and the girls loved it.

For me, happiness in motherhood was found in the small moments: private moments together over breakfast, sharing their day after school, sitting at the kitchen table doing homework, or talking and laughing as we prepared dinner. We often sat long after the meal was over, listening to Don's baby stories from labor and delivery. At times, the girls would gross out at the details, running away from the table then quickly coming back for the big question: "Was it a girl or a boy?!"

I loved our moments before bedtime with homework complete, chores finished, as we shared their day. I would read them "book stories," but the best nights were when Don would tell them "his bedtime stories." He had a bag full of stories he made up as he went along, weaving and creating wonderful adventures. "The Centipede's Shoes" was one of their favorites, telling of the centipede that went to the town shoemaker. Thirty-five pairs of legs created quite a challenge for the little town shoemaker! Shannon loved this story so much that she wrote the story out and illustrated it herself, saving it to one day read to her children. Meghan wanted to make a play out of it for Shannon and her friends to act out, accomplishing the task before winter.

These special, seemingly small moments make up the joyful, precious memories of parenthood. The laughs, the love, the play, and the hugs are woven together for all eternity. They fortify us as parents for days to come when our children begin the journey into a world beyond our home.

THE JOY OF MOTHERHOOD

Perhaps more than any other time, early motherhood expands our capacity for love, joy, and personal growth—for us, for our children, and for our husbands. We all do life better when supported by others. My mom-friends and I met once a week for our stitchery night. We made quilts, knitted baby blankets, needlepointed pillows, or made decoupage Christmas ornaments. One friend knitted a twelve-foot scarf for over a year because she didn't know how to end it! I loved the encouragement and support for one another. Many of us forged friendships lasting to this day.

Don and I also had the love and support of our family. My sisters, their families, and our parents were together often, celebrating birthdays and other milestones. In this spring of our married life, Don and I lived each day to the fullest. We entertained family and opened our doors to wonderful, new neighbors. We formed a close group with four to five couples, those mentioned in the previous Stone. The men loved to eat and all of us gals loved to cook and entertain, so we met for a dinner group once a month. We took turns hosting, with each occasion becoming a special memory.

Shannon and Meghan's friends at school were also their year-round friends in our neighborhood. All the kids could safely walk to school together and stop for snacks at Zietan's family grocery store on the way home. In the summer, just like my own childhood, we told our children to "come home when the streetlights come on."

We spent our recreation time together at the Yacht Club. Several of us would pack the galley in our sailboats with food and appetizers and sail to Catalina to enjoy the beautiful weather for a few days every three or four weeks. The Yacht Club had

"One of the deep secrets
of life is that all
that is really worth doing
is what we do for others."

— Lewis Carroll

activities for all ages and occasions—women's luncheons, birthday luncheons, after-church luncheons, and dinner events for couples every weekend. The kids kept busy with Swim Team and Sabot Sailing Regattas as the Club allowed us all to enjoy nature in her most spectacular attire. Sailboats with crisp, white sails still tied down would slowly make their way to the jetty, gliding on the pristine, blue water that glistened with sparkles of sunlight. I can still smell the clean, fresh ocean breeze mixed with the pungent aroma of gasoline engines.

Don was most happy when at the helm of our sailboat, family in tow and opera music blaring from below. Once out past the jetty and into open water, he loved to catch a sail and go fast—so fast I would grab the girls and hold onto them for dear life, yelling for him to slow down before he lost one of us! One Sunday as we were returning home, the ocean was so choppy and the wind so strong that Captain Bligh ordered me take down the Spinnaker sail before it capsized us. As I crawled to the bow, the boat pitched to the right and I suddenly found myself half-dangling off the boat, hanging onto the mainmast with all my strength. Don told Shannon to take the wheel while he rescued me. Fortunately, we didn't have to call on seven-year old Meghan to help with the rescue mission! It made for a good ocean tale.

Every Sunday during the summer we enjoyed concerts in the park along the ocean wall not far from our house. We would appear at three o'clock sharp, laden with chairs, blankets, carafes of lemonade, thermoses of coffee, everyone's choice of wine, and enough food to feed ourselves as well as the band. It was the best band music—loud and robust with flutes, oboes, clarinets, trombones, trumpets, cymbals, and drums. Kids marched around the park and played on the grass, with us sharing good laughs and warm, genuine friendship. Our dinners were gourmet, each of us making one or two delectable dishes we shared with one another. After a few summers, we had all enlarged our recipe files and epicurean talents.

HIS GOODNESS : SHARED FATHERING

Shannon and Meghan's father, Chuck, was part of their lives on a weekly basis. Each Sunday, Chuck picked them up at eleven thirty in the morning and spent the day with them until seven o'clock in the evening. Often Chuck would arrive early and join us in the kitchen for a cup of coffee. While the girls finished getting ready, we shared thoughts on how the girls were doing in their new life. Don and I were always home relaxing when they came home in the evening. I often gave them time and space before going up to help them get ready for bed. We never questioned them on aspects of their dad's life that were none of our business, and Chuck never pried for information the girls did not offer.

That's not to say it was easy for any of us, especially the girls. Don and I, as well as Chuck, were still in monthly counseling with the same counselor to ensure we did what was best for the girls. We included Chuck in special events as he wanted, whether school sports, ballet programs, or school performances. After a time, Chuck remarried, and these times became less frequent, but he remained a strong, weekly presence in the girls' lives.

SCHOOL DAYS

Having thrown my entire self into the girls' early years, I was not prepared for the loss I experienced when I took my youngest daughter to her first year of elementary school. With Meghan in first grade and Shannon in fifth, I was alone all day. The empty house felt unbearable to me. Several of my friends filled their days with substitute teaching, earning advanced college degrees, or returning to the workforce.

CORONA DEL MAR DAYS

Homeschooling children had not yet entered the mainstream, or I would have loved utilizing my training as a teacher to do so.

I volunteered to be Room Mother for both girls, became their Brownie and Girl Scout Troop Co-Leader, took up tennis lessons and played doubles with friends, and joined a women's volunteer organization. But I still had gifts and talents that were calling out to be used. I had always worked, and I missed being around people every day. I considered teaching Lamaze again, but that would require being gone at night, which was precious time with my family. I wanted something that would be close to home, but get me out of the house and use my creative talents.

MY WILLIAM ERNEST BROWN DAYS

My favorite store sold custom invitations and stationery design and was owned by two women, Eileen and Diane, whom I loved as much as the shop and its products. I asked if they would mind if I opened a franchise across the bay, a good distance from their store. They gave me the name of Bill Brown, owner of the Franchise of William Ernest Brown, Stationers. He had about thirty stores across the country in addition to his parent store in Beverly Hills. Soon I was on my way to being a business owner! One of my Lamaze training classmates begged me to bring her in as a partner. It seemed a good idea at the time: we could share the financial investment as well as the daytime hours of retail. We signed a ten-year lease.

My husband and daughters were excited for me to have a small business just ten minutes from our home. Our beautiful store opened in 1980, filled with everything associated with a desk, letter, and journal writing—beautifully engraved correspondence stationery and an array of ribbons, papers, and typestyles for every imaginable custom design, and dozens of catalogs for non-custom orders.

We did every kind of invitation and announcement for any kind of event. The shop featured unique touches for women who understood the handwritten gift of a letter—personalized correspondence cards, informal notes, fountain pens, sealing wax, imported Italian leather and marbled paper planning agendas, photo albums, and beautiful gifts galore to embrace and share the gift of friendship, with comfortable sofas and large coffee tables around which to design our best creations. We served coffee in the morning and tea in the afternoon, with sweets and treats offered amidst beautiful music. It was truly a delightful, alive place to shop.

Our friends became our employees. Charlotte and Sally did beautiful calligraphy and design, while Irma, Ruth, Sandy, and Nancy added their own sense of creative chic, panache, and style. We loved sharing all things beautiful, all joyful expressions of love and friendship. For evenings, summer and Christmas season, we added bright, creative college students, who enlarged our team with fresh, fun, youthful energy. The seventy-year-old mother-in-law of one of my needlepoint friends wanted to work in our store a few hours a day. Fran was a jewel and became our grand dame. I worked from when the girls went to school at eight o'clock until about three o'clock in the afternoon when I picked them up. Fran came to work at two o'clock, working until closing. Not only did I love and rely on her, but the customers also loved her easygoing manner while the rest of us bustled around. She had a calming effect on all of us, with a great sense of humor and wit. Fran worked with us for ten wonderful years. We were one

"A letter is a gift

we give ourselves."

— *Alexandra Stoddard,*
Gift of a Letter

big, happy family. Often, I would take the girls back to the shop after school to do their homework and visit with the gals. They loved being a part of the fun and choosing an after-school treat at the local ice cream shop.

It was the most delightful business to own! I loved the challenge of teambuilding, teaching, training, and learning in all areas of creative design. We had tremendous perks! Each January, husbands and wives were invited for a spectacular weekend with William Brown and Company in their beautiful home in Big Sur, California. Each spring, we traveled to New York City with other franchise owners for the New York Stationery Show, with private showings with exclusive custom vendors in beautiful hotels and venues in NYC. We worked hard all day, ate epicurean dinners at night and took in as many Broadway shows as twelve days would allow! We also traveled for buying trips throughout the year to Dallas and Atlanta. But what I loved most of all was working with people I loved as a team to make a beautiful, fun, resourceful place where our creative gifts and talents could please our clients. We helped educate our clients on the beauty of design and etiquette in all manners of invitations and correspondence. We were the Emily Post and Letitia Baldrige of the paper world! Our customers became our loyal patrons and friends.

Perhaps this is what our shop was all about: providing a way to reach out and touch others with our hearts of friendship. I've loved books since I can remember. I've loved beautiful small treasures from my daughters on my nightstand, a fresh flower in my MacKenzie-Childs vase on my desk, the new or musty smell of the paper of the book in my hand, the fragrance of ink in a fountain pen as it glides with words to lift the spirits of a friend on beautiful, smooth paper, and connecting with those we love, all brought deep joy and satisfaction to me. Having a shop filled with all things beautiful provided others with ideas of connecting from their hearts to others.

"Letters mingle souls."

— *John Donne*

Never forsake the art of letter writing. Being a Woman of Letters is still one of the most beautiful expressions of ourselves we can give to others. They live on long after we are gone. I've kept all my letters from my children, family, and close friends in beautiful marbled paper boxes I've collected over my years of buying for the shop.

A FORK IN THE ROAD

There was just one problem—after the first wild, demanding Christmas season in retail, my partner "just didn't think it was fun anymore." She wanted out of our agreement! Not only did she want out, she also wanted her investment back, because she had taken it out of her husband's retirement fund!

Dear Reader, I confess that my stubbornness reared its head. I had no intention of failing in this endeavor, nor was I a quitter! A close attorney friend offered to give his advice, for free. To prevent having to reimburse my partner, he suggested that I, too, walk away from the lease agreement while I was ahead. He warned it would be a heavy burden for me to maintain the financial and physical responsibility on my own. I labored over what to do.

Hindsight tells me perhaps I should have run. Today I see that my commitment to my family does and should have priority over a commitment to the lease owner. However, with that aside, I believed I was in the perfect place at the time, being able to work the hours when my children were in school. I've always thrived in motivating environments. Knowing how much I loved having the shop and believing in my business sense, my husband encouraged me to keep our investment in the store. We reimbursed my partner's share of the investment and carried on alone.

That decision was a major fork in my life's road. At times, I wondered what

my life and my family's life would have been like had I walked away. Many, many times when things got rough and I was working sixteen-hour days during the Christmas holidays, I regretted my decision.

Our shop was wonderfully successful, having nine part-time women and students forming our team of associates. We helped one another with conflicting family schedules and encouraged each other to keep our lives in balance. However, I can honestly remember sitting at my desk at home on Sunday afternoons when the girls were with their dad, thinking, "My life is totally out of balance!" Either my family was doing great and my business was paying the price, or my business was doing great and my husband and daughters were paying the price. More accurately, everything and everyone was doing fine except me! I was the one missing out, failing to savor this season of life. I didn't want my girls or Don to miss out, so I ran myself ragged, striving to do all things perfectly and lovingly.

I was convinced I could have it all—family and career. To be candid, I took it as a challenge to prove I could do it all, and do it with great aplomb. From my perspective now, I realize it's a lie. We can't have it all. We must make trade-offs and be intentional to keep our balance. Someone once shared these wise words with me: "Know which balls you are juggling that cannot be broken—the glass balls of marriage and family."

HIS KINDNESS : A NEW HOME AND AN ANGEL SIGHTING

One beautiful spring afternoon, as Don and I drove down the California coast enjoying the blue skies, turquoise ocean water, and white sailboats bobbing like toothpicks on the horizon, we spotted a "For Sale" sign. Without a word, Don made a quick right turn off Pacific Coast Highway into a lovely enclave of homes called Shorecliffs. There we first saw our beloved Driftwood Road home. We fell in love with the charm and personality of this house nestled among beautiful birch trees. A beckoning gate led to an outdoor patio, with the house encircling it, French doors opening onto it from every room. The house became a spiritual Godsend. God had quite a life in store for all of us in this lovely Corona del Mar Village, which truly was the "Crown of the Sea."

Shortly after our move, a gal introduced herself after church as Jill and welcomed us to the area. She asked if I would like to go to a Bible study that week. She had no idea I had been praying for a Bible study! That Wednesday, Jill and I drove to Laguna Beach for the study. We walked into a sanctuary full of four hundred or more women chatting and laughing together. Another friend of mine spotted me and we sat together, both laughing as we compared our new, shiny, gold-edged Bibles. All the other women were carrying well-worn Bibles, indicating their familiarity with God's Word. The Catholic Daily Missal had included Scripture and prayer, but I had never owned a complete Bible until then, with new shiny gold indexed pages. I was quite excited and eager to learn how to study God's Word.

God had led me to Bible Study Fellowship (BSF), an international Christian inter-denominational fellowship, offering an organized and disciplined system for the study of the Scriptures. Each study lasts nine months, and over a nine-year cycle, the curriculum covers Genesis, the Life of Moses, Isaiah, Israel and the Minor Prophets, Matthew, John, Acts of the Apostles, Romans, and Revelation. I was so happy to have found it.

As I left the church, I searched everywhere for Jill to thank her for this incredible answer to prayer. I couldn't find her—and I never did see her again. I looked for her everywhere, but no one at BSF or at our church knew of anyone named Jill.

I concluded God had sent a messenger to me—an angel assigned to lead me to

Come to Me, all who are weary and heavy-laden,
and I will give you rest.
Take My yoke upon you, and learn from Me,
for I am gentle and humble in heart;
and you shall find rest for your souls.
For My yoke is easy, and My load is light.

— Matthew 11:28-30

Him and His Word. It was both a humbling and grateful conclusion.

Each and every Wednesday, six of us met for an hour before BSF, enjoying cups of C'est Si Bon lattes. Before long, we began to share our concerns with each other and pray for one another. The confidence and love that grew among that group of prayer sisters was extremely satisfying to us all. Some thirty years later, Donna, Yvonne, and I are still prayer sisters. The rest have gone on to be with the Lord.

At the same time, our freshman daughter Meghan expressed a desire to attend a nondenominational church with a strong youth group that several of her friends attended. Since our Catholic church did not have much to offer teenagers, we decided to give it a try. The rest is history. This church was alive and overflowing with warm community and the Holy Spirit. We met so many people in a short amount of time who were in love with the Lord, wanting to serve others and make a difference in their Kingdom Calling. These were the first steps on my path toward a spiritual reawakening.

HIS CALLING : ENCOUNTER WITH THE HOUND OF HEAVEN

It was the perfect time for God's hand to move. I was being pressed on all sides by the challenges of parenting teenagers, struggling to give up control as my precious daughters expanded their lives away from our family kitchen table. Add to this the pressures of my business, as well as the cultural expectations of peer and social groups, and I felt as though I were in a vice. Perhaps you've felt these pressures, too? Don and I shared a growing frustration with our lifestyle. We constantly lived under the demands of both our work schedules. Our family was living life in the fast lane. We were exhausted, frustrated, overwhelmed, and spiritually depleted—and we knew it.

Motherhood and fatherhood can bring us to our knees. The fruit of parenthood is not only the legacy of our children; it also produces fruit in us as mothers and fathers. It changes, transforms, and awakens the craving for God in our lives.

My spiritual awakening and rededication to the Lord came on a beautiful summer morning on my knees beside the bed on the seventh floor of the Maui Hyatt Regency Hotel in Hawaii. I was physically, emotionally, and spiritually spent. I watched as through a kaleidoscope as my forty-three years turned before my eyes. I confessed my sins as quickly as they were revealed and sensed God was calling me in a new direction, away from the busy, hurried nature of our lives. I could not ignore His compelling voice in my spirit.

The greatest treasures entrusted to me by the Lord were my daughters, Shannon and Meghan. God had given them beautiful spirits, big hearts, gifts, and talents. I wanted nothing more than for God to do His will in their lives. So very slowly as I knelt in that room, I imagined taking a deep pink ribbon for Shannon and a pale pink one for Meghan, and slowly wrapping each one, from the bottom of their toes to the top of their head, praying for every aspect of their lives as I went. When I reached the top of their heads, I tied a great big bow and offered them to the Lord. I promised Him, from that day forward, I would watch to see what His purpose was for each of their lives and do everything I could to grow them according to it.

It's been said that "A daughter is a mother's heart walking outside of her body." I gave my daughters into God's Perfect Hands.

Motherhood taught me how to be a prayer warrior, seeking God's mercy and grace in all humility as I brought my petitions before the Lord. I began bringing my children before Him each day.

How tenderly the Lord welcomes our cries! He was teaching me to listen to Him as we walked our girls through the changing landscape and potential minefields of their teenage and young adult years. Renewed and refreshed in my spiritual walk, I felt prepared to be used by God for His purpose in the next season of life.

Be anxious for nothing, but in everything by prayer and supplication
with thanksgiving let your requests be made known to God.
And the peace of God, which surpasses all comprehension,
shall guard your hearts and your minds in Christ Jesus.
Finally, brethren, whatever is true, whatever is honorable,
whatever is right, whatever is pure, whatever is lovely,
whatever is of good repute, if there is any excellence
and anything worthy of praise, let your mind dwell on these things.

— *Philippians 4:6-8*

With the continued weekly study of God's Word in Bible Study Fellowship, my spiritual discipline and obedience grew and I began to see the world through God's eyes. I continued to grow closer to Him in my daily prayer time and grew in knowledge of Him daily in His Word through this intensive study. The teaching and fellowship of our new church community led our family to step away from the Catholic Church. We all agreed we had come home in this ecumenical Christian Church. While we've embraced a new journey and personal expression of worshipping the Father, Son, and Holy Spirit, I am forever grateful for the deep, meditative prayer life and strong, disciplined traditions that I learned growing up in the Catholic Church. They remain with me today in all I do.

RIPENING FRUIT OF MIDDLE MOTHERHOOD

The hurried life of the hurried child in junior high and high school brought its own challenges. My relationship with my daughters became more stretched as they struggled to grow and become young adults in the public school environment. At the same time, my husband was panicking over the short time that remained before the girls took off for college.

He began planning great family trips as time and finances permitted. We skied in the winter and vacationed at the beach in the summer. We stepped up our cultural experiences with Broadway shows in New York and explored our American heritage in Washington, D.C. We visited the Smithsonian and as many landmarks as we could, while laughing about the girls thinking a trip to the National Mall meant a day of shopping! Instead they experienced firsthand the immense cost of war and other atrocities, the historical impact of our Founding Fathers and the Constitution, and the impressive wisdom those men brought forth with their commitment to our nation.

One of our most memorable trips was spending two weeks of Christmas vacation in London and Paris. The girls were the perfect age at sixteen and eighteen. We jammed all we could into a week in each city. In London, we visited Buckingham Palace, Parliament, museums, and restaurants galore. We saw the London premiere of Cats and, two nights later, the West End City premiere of Les Miserables. We'll never forget shopping at Harrods the day after Christmas with each girl choosing a special gift to remember our time abroad.

Paris was rainy and cold, but nothing could dampen our spirits as we walked the streets, ducking into every shop that held anything feminine. All the shops had beautifully decorated Christmas Trees on the outside of the store as well as the inside

Train up a child in the way he should go:

Even when he is old he will not depart from it.

— Proverbs 22:6

with no expense spared to celebrate the season. We visited all the beautiful, historical landmarks, the most memorable being The Louvre and Notre Dame. We loved the little villages, narrow streets, and tiny shops, with Christmas cheer and hot tea and cider pouring into each of us, warming our cold bodies. The finale of our trip was a New Year's Eve dinner cruise down the River Seine, all dressed in our finest attire. Don wore his suit and overcoat; the girls wore their prettiest dresses and coats; and I wore my blue wool dress with a black silk waistband under my favorite coat. It was a magical, divine evening. After the cruise was over, we rushed over to the Arc de Triomphe in the rush to celebrate the New Year—1985. It was a spectacle of sight and sound with the best hot chocolate ever!

But the excitement of the night was not over. Unable to hail a taxi, we began our hike home in freezing temperatures and with the girls in high heels. Before we knew it, Don was snatched from our arms by a band of gypsies who tried to strip him of his watch, wallet, and coat! We hit them with our brand new Paris handbags, yelling and screaming for help. After fighting his way out of the pile, Don thanked us for saving his life as he thought they wanted more than his belongings. We continued on as Shannon could barely walk in her three-inch heels. I no sooner had exchanged my low heels for her high heels, when a taxi driver, having pity upon seeing a freezing family, stopped and offered us a ride. However, the rules were only three people to a taxi. It was so cold we told Shannon and Meghan to take the taxi, and we would meet them back at the hotel, praying for another taxi! They jumped into the warm taxi with big smiles of relief on their faces as I looked down and realized I still had the three-inch heels on my aching feet! We had several stories to tell when we returned home!

HIS ANOINTING : FOREVER MOTHERHOOD

With my daughters grown and on their own, as wives and mothers, I am so proud and thankful of who they are and how much they love and are blessed by the Lord.

I celebrate you, my daughters, and your lives today, thankful for how the Lord has blessed you with gifts and talents to serve your husbands and children, as well as other young people who find love and encouragement being in your presence, as you pour yourselves into serving your family. I am so very proud and grateful for the beautiful women you are today, loving wives, moms and daughters, strong and stalwart, faithful to the Lord

I look back now and reflect on God's faithfulness, love, mercy, and grace during those motherhood years. Fortunately, Motherhood never ends. What a blessing that we are mothers forever—only with changing roles! When the girls were in college, I always made home a safe place to land. I called them the "airport years," coming home for a landing, getting refueled, then being fortified to take off again for their adventures. It was always special having them call and ask if they could fly or drive home for the weekend. I spoiled them with home-cooked meals, family time and shopping!

When they were newly married, I rejoiced when they came home, fussed over them, and prepared their favorite meals. I tried to treat them as treasured guests, not children. I didn't expect them to carry on the responsibilities in the kitchen they had as children; helping to serve the meal, helping to clear or to wash the dishes! We loved our dinner time sharing more than ever. We had a tradition of "Sunday Night Suppers," when we would invite friends to share family time.

Motherhood is forever. We change with the needs of our children, being quiet when they don't seek our input, speaking honestly with love when they seek our advice, and sometimes just listening while they talk it out themselves. We encourage and support them, loving them unconditionally in the process. I believe this is what God desires of us: to grow in love, tenderly creating a lifelong circle of giving and receiving love with our children. And above all, we continue to "pray without ceasing" (1 Thess. 5:17). We have the assurance of God's faithfulness and strong hand being with us in the battle for the souls of our children. A mother is a prayer warrior forever!

*Therefore, since we are surrounded by such a huge crowd
of witnesses to the life of faith,
let us strip off every weight that slows us down,
especially the sin that so easily trips us up.
And let us run with endurance the race God has set before us.
We do this by keeping our eyes on Jesus,
the champion who initiates and perfects our faith.*

— Hebrews 12:1-2

HIS I AM : OUR GREAT CLOUD OF WITNESSES

Along our journey, we have known and unknown heroes who've walked before us, passing on the baton of God's faithfulness!

OUR ABRAHAM, the father of our faith who never wavered in his trust in God's Promises to him, that He would make a mighty nation of Abraham's descendants.

Abraham prayed for his children, as we also pray for our children and our children's children.

OUR MOSES, who faithfully prayed and interceded for his people (those who God entrusted to him) when they were needy, unbelieving and complaining, worshipping false idols, especially when God was angry and wanted to destroy them and wipe them from earth for their disobedience and rebellion. Moses prayed. He persevered in prayer until the end of his life! The life of Moses reminds us that life is not free of problems, conflicts, and heartaches. The best preparation we can give our children for facing hardships is prayer and God's Word. Our commitment to prayer for our children is a main part of forever motherhood for which there is no stopping on this side of heaven.

OUR JOSHUA, our divinely anointed and prepared leader to bring the Israelites into the Promised Land, with God's presence, protection, provision, and His all-powerful faithfulness. As we wrestle with our idols of busyness and perfection, allowing others to define us, JOSHUA reminds us to receive the baton from our mothers and fathers to us and pass it to our children and grandchildren with God's caution and command to follow Him alone.

OUR PSALMS AND PROVERBS, where David and others pour out their hearts to the Lord. We follow their example, continually bringing our needs before the Lord; awakening our Spirit with shouts, cries, and acclamations; surrendering all thoughts and emotions to our Father, the Hound of Heaven; crying out for our hearts to be filled by Him as we pray without ceasing.

Do not remember the former things,
Nor consider the things of old.
Behold, I will do a new thing,
Now it shall spring forth;
Shall you not know it?
I will even make a road in the wilderness
And rivers in the desert.

— Isaiah 43:18

OUR DEAR ISAIAH, who so tenderly records the words of the LORD:

Do not fear, for I have redeemed you;
I have called you by name; you are Mine!
When you pass through the waters,
I will be with you;
And through the rivers, they will not overflow you.
When you walk through the fire, you will not be scorched,
Nor will the flame burn you.
For I am the Lord your God, The Holy One of Israel, your Savior...
Do not fear, for I am with you.

— *Isaiah 43:1-3,5*

During one of the lowest moments of my life, one Sunday when I could barely bring my body to church, the Lord so graciously and mercifully gave that Scripture in the Sermon. It flew like an arrow into my soul, piercing the darkness. For the first time in many months, it renewed my hope and faith in such a way that it burst forth brighter than the sunlight streaming through the windows. Keep praying!

OUR JEREMIAH, our reminder that God is with us all throughout our years of motherhood. What assurance!

OUR JESUS CHRIST, our Lord and Savior, our Light, Truth, and Life. He is our all.

For I know the plans I have for you,
plans for your welfare, not for disaster.

— *Jeremiah 29:11*

REFLECTIONS ON MOTHERHOOD

Motherhood is filled with moments of struggle and sacrifice, but these are sandwiched between tremendous moments of unbelievable joy! This is how we travel this Motherhood Stone, failing to remember the trials, instead, celebrating the joys. Like Mary, we treasure up all these things and ponder them in our hearts (Luke 2:19).

My dearest daughters, this Stone has been a joy for me to write. Mothering is so dear to my heart, overflowing with love for each of you. It's been nearly impossible to choose what memories to put on the written page. I am abundantly grateful for the blessing and privilege I have being your mother in God's eternal plan. I will return to motherhood again as we navigate the waters ahead.

For now, let me call us to reflect, thank the Lord, and celebrate our children. In whatever season of motherhood you find yourself today, whether in the future or the past, whether you mother your own biological children or another's, all motherhood is a reason to rejoice. Our children are our greatest legacy we offer to the Lord, a valuable and precious legacy that goes far beyond this life and on into eternity. May God be forever near you as you pursue the high calling of motherhood.

GRACE NOTES | *Motherhood*

- Give thanks, always, for God's incredible gift to you of your children.

- Motherhood and fatherhood enlarges our hearts in ways we never expected. It expands to make room for the love of sacrifice and surrender to the needs of our children each and every child, and then balloons to love all our children's spouses and our phenomenal grandchildren!

- The river of motherhood moves swiftly. Reach out and capture each drop of water, each special moment, not only the special events, but the quiet moments, as well.

- As women and mothers, we have to constantly strive to keep our priorities straight. In God's world, it's God first, family second, and all else third. Use that as your grid.

- Make memories! When given the choice of staying home or making a memory, jump in the car and go!

- Establish traditions. It gives stability and security to your family's days and creates anticipation of precious family time.

- Celebrate one another's achievements and goals. Encourage and lift each other up with spirit and enthusiasm.

- Become a prayer warrior for your children and your family. Ask how you can pray for them, what are their special needs, etc., then take it to God in prayer. Refer to Stone 1 Grace Notes.

- The greatest gift you can give your child is unconditional love—true, wrapping-your arms-around-them-no-matter-what, unconditional love. No matter the disagreements or differences, strive to maintain a great relationship with each of your children.

- My daughters and daughters-in-law have been a tremendous help in our "stepping through" the minefields of adult mother/daughter relationships. We love one another and give each other grace.

- Think of your family and friend relationships as your treasured garden. Water and fertilize generously; take out the weeds as they pop up, spend time enjoying the beauty and uniqueness of each single flower, and thank God for His Creation!

- Be generous in all ways, with all your heart, time, and prayers.

Greater love has no one than this,
that someone lay down his life for his friends.

— *John 15:12-13*

STONE 6   SEASONS OF FRIENDSHIP

*D*ue to a leader's illness, two small groups in our Bible Study Fellowship had been combined for a day—a young mothers group and our "more mature" grandmothers group. We had just closed our seating circle to better hear one another when a young mom and her baby quietly opened the door, ushering in the cold, blustery wind and rain. She sat in the chair closest to the door, outside of our circle.

"Oh, come in with us," said the leader, "and welcome!"

"Oh, this is fine," she softly replied. "I have my baby sleeping in the stroller."

"Well, we'll all hear the baby if he needs you, which is just fine with us, so please, bring your chair into our circle so we can share motherhood with you."

"My name is Kaitlin," she smiled and moved to a chair within our circle. "Thank you." My eyes filled with tears, a seemingly silly response to this lovely young mother. BSF hasn't changed, I thought to myself, always caring and inclusive, encouraging and enlisting the love of Christ from all of us.

After discussing John 11 about the raising of Lazarus from the dead, when Jesus arrives two days "late," the leader asked a question of the group. Can you remember a time when Jesus waited to answer your prayer, and what did you learn about Him in that experience?"

Kaitlin raised her hand as she answered. "Being a new mother has really challenged me with feelings of isolation and loneliness. My mom passed way a few years ago, and I'm so lost without her here to help me. I had been praying for a friend and role model and when someone invited me to join Bible Study Fellowship a few months ago, I learned that God is faithful."

Need I tell you how quiet that room became as her words so tenderly spilled onto the floor? Driving home after class, I realized why she had touched my heart. I related to her because of the loss of my mom when I was only nineteen. I felt the wound of isolation, loneliness, inadequacy—not only the loss of my role model, but my greatest cheerleader. I thanked God for bringing Kaitlin to our class that day and for showing all of us the difference we could make in people's lives when we choose to love like Jesus. We're all called to join the inner circle of His love.

FRIENDSHIP QUILTS

In the "good ol' days," my grandmother spent most of her adult life with other women in a quilting bee, cutting and stitching beautiful remnants of fabric into legacy quilts for newlyweds and new mothers. They would stitch and tell stories, sharing their journey through motherhood. She was also involved in knitting and dressmaking circles, as well as food-preservation groups where she and the other ladies had the opportunity to work together and share life together.

My mother and friends worked hard in the housekeeping role of the 40s. Chores were more difficult to manage, from laundry down in the cold basement, hanging clothes out to dry on the clothesline before they froze at dusk, shoveling coal into the furnace several times a day to stay warm, cooking all the meals from scratch, with food and supplies being rationed, sewing and mending clothes in their spare time, all the while wearing dresses, heels, and lipstick! The mothers

My grandmother Catherine, with my mother Dorothy

in the neighborhood met in one another's home for coffee-klatch's, their times of 'chatting over coffee' almost daily. Most families only had one car, which was used by the husband to drive to work. When the wife needed the car for grocery shopping or errands, it meant driving her husband to and from work each day.

In the 1970s, when my daughters were young, most of my friends and I met through preschool, play groups, Brownies, and Girl Scouts:

"Make new friends but keep the old,
one is silver and the other is gold."

As our children grew older, we had beach days in the summer with swim team at the pool, while winter found us connecting with one another by sitting on the sidelines at soccer games. Later on, when our kids were in middle and high school, book clubs, dinner groups, Bible studies, and church ministry filled our days. Young moms today tell me most of their friendships began from preschool and MOPS (Mothers of Preschoolers), church groups, work out classes, coffee and lunch dates, social media, job and career circles, Bible studies and church ministry. So things aren't really all that different. One thing is sure. We need to make the time and give ourselves permission to take the time to cultivate precious friendships.

WE ARE WIRED FOR INTIMACY

As I shared with you in Stone 1, my first memory of having a best friend, other than my cousins, was in sixth grade on the cold Wisconsin ice-skating rink. Marline and I have traversed all of our stones in the river together, even though we haven't lived in the same state for fifty years! The stones in our river have been placed before each of us in a different pattern, yet we share the joys and travails with each other. And even though our lives have taken us in very different directions, we can call each other and pick up right where we left off. I love that we shared those fifteen years of our youth, cementing us together through all of life. We had a very strong core group of friends throughout high school and many of us have managed to gather together for most of our high school reunions—including our 50th!

OUR FABULOUS 40s & 50s

By the time I reached "middle motherhood"—what I like to call the years of parenting junior high and high school age children—I was in my forties, thought I knew everything, and felt my life had accelerated into high speed. My husband and daughters called for me at home and school, my business was growing by leaps and bounds, and God was blessing me with wonderful friendships in our church and women's ministries. Before long, several friends and I were leading the women's ministry groups, chairing the annual Women's Retreat, founding Heart to Heart (Titus 2, proclaiming older women to become mentors to younger women), and acting as a member of Women's Council and the Women's Executive Board. We joined with other churches to present Christian Leadership Week. Several women in the city would volunteer their homes and gifts of hospitality for an open house each spring coinciding with the Mayor's Prayer Breakfast, where speakers gave testimony to their relationship with Jesus Christ.

As I entered my fifties, it was a dream come true to have Shannon work alongside me in Long Beach. Meghan was in her first year of college at the University of Oregon, and her absence left a big void in our home. Steve and Shannon (married two years earlier) had transferred from San Luis Obispo to the University of California, Irvine, to complete their degrees and lived in an apartment near our home. Each day,

Shannon and I drove the hour round-trip to work together, planning and designing as we went. She was such a natural at color and design that the clients loved her. She fit right in with our staff, because she knew all my friends who had worked in the shop since the beginning.

Each and every person made a great contribution to the success of the store. The demanding reality of retail was that for two months out of the year we worked twelve-hour days at the shop. Shannon and I then came home and worked another four hours on the art and design work for our clients' large, custom Christmas card orders. It was grueling and demanding, yet all was forgotten after the clients' praise, jubilation, and gratitude when they picked them up!

Even during the most demanding month of retail business, we managed to carry on one of our most treasured traditions—our annual Mother-Daughter Christmas Tea, held the first Sunday of December. Sally and her daughter Katy, along with Shannon, Meghan, and me, took turns hosting the event in our homes while all of us baked, cooked, and prepared the feast. I can still picture that first year, when our girls were young, with a "Teddy Bear Christmas" theme. All the decorations were matching-teddy-bear everything—including our aprons!

We loved setting up the children's tables with their own special treats and decorations. Mothers not only brought their daughters, but often their mother, sister, aunt, or grandmother. The gathering grew every year! The children brought ornaments for a gift exchange with each other, as well as a children's gift to donate to Angel Tree Christmas—a ministry to children of prisoners and their families. We always ended the day around our piano singing Christmas carols. The girls and their friends sang the loudest. It was a delightful and lovely

celebration of friendship—a tradition we continued with our daughters, their friends, and their mothers well into their high school and college years.

HIS FAITHFULNESS : OUR KINGDOM WORK

In 1990, we opened our beautiful new location in Newport Beach, JO KING & CO. in the chic area of Westcliff Court. Reflecting on those busy retail years in our shop, I see much of what we gave our clients was friendship, warm hospitality, beautiful music, teaching and design, along with encouragement and inspiration to express themselves to give to those they love. It gave me such pleasure to have Shannon learn the business and enjoy the perks of ownership. We looked forward to the day Meghan could join us.

In the spring of 1993, Shannon and I went to NYC a few days early for a much-needed rest before the strenuous week of the trade show in our thirteenth year. Shannon was pregnant and experiencing morning sickness. Don and I couldn't wait to be grandparents! Here's what I wrote in my journal:

> *"I was awakened the entire night, while Shannon slept. My mind was filled with strong visual pictures, like those in a kaleidoscope, each picture a quick snapshot as the result of having my shop. This continued the entire four nights, leaving me anxious and unsettled. I was left with several messages. God's wish for me is NOT to continue having the shop. It has taken over my life, Shannon's life, and everyone's in our family, for it has interrupted true family life."*

God showed me my first obligation was to Him and to my husband and family—emotionally and physically. And I so wanted to have time to be a Grandmother!

The decision was made to close the store in February after the next Christmas season. While I felt tremendous peace with my decision, I dreaded the thought of closing my beautiful dream, missing our incredible clients who I cared for as friends. But most of all, I didn't want to lose the faithful friendships of those who had worked for me so many years. Yet I could not pretend I did not know what God had made clear to me.

JOURNAL ENTRY: 1993

Let it be written here, that one of the most important reasons I am closing the store is because of the strong wrestling matches I had with the Holy Spirit last May, 1993, with one clear, unmistakable message: Get out of the store, Jo, and get out now. Being obedient to You, Lord, even when my mind conjures up so many valid reasons to stay, is so difficult for me, Lord…but I do it in FAITH.

We had so many "friendship" visits the last month; everyone was so very sad to see us closing.

There were so many beautiful encounters for all of us in the shop today… so many customers having as hard of a time of this as we are. No price tag high enough could ever have been placed on their FRIENDSHIP and LOVE for us!!

The shop had been a perfect fit for me. I went through a tough time after we closed. It felt like I had been in a wonderful circus tent with people all around, when the center pole had collapsed and everyone escaped—except me. Little did I know that God was preparing me for my world to fall apart. God always goes before us.

As iron sharpens iron,
so one person sharpens another.

— *Proverbs 27:17*

THE BEAUTIFUL FACE OF FRIENDSHIP

Look in the mirror. What do you see? Look past the tired eyes, increasing wrinkles, insecurities, fears, doubt, and self-effacement. What do your friends see?

To our friends, our faces are the beautiful faces of friendship.

A dear, longtime family friend and I had lost touch with one another through a time of mutual, hurtful misunderstanding some eighteen years ago at the time of this writing. I knew she and her husband had retired in a small ocean town. I had discovered her whereabouts through the forwarding address on her Christmas card. Our annual family photographs and personal notes kept each other up-to-date, promising to make the time to see one another the following year. Two years ago, her beautifully hand-painted Christmas card included a note of her husband's passing. I wanted to run to her and wrap my arms around her. I had no phone number, nor could I find anyone who did. I promptly sent her a note, giving my phone number and asking if she would please share hers as well. She did. But when I called her she did not respond to my numerous calls. I had forgiven her part, I thought, but obviously she had not forgiven mine. We kept in touch with a few more Christmas cards and personal notes, enjoying updates on our families.

Recently, however, I knew I would be in her area. I took a deep breath, said a short prayer, and called her number. Once again, she didn't answer. Shall I leave a message? I smiled as I heard her voice recording and forged ahead, unable to stop smiling as I left mine just moments before heading into the Santa Rosa mountain range where I would have no cell coverage on my phone!

Two days later, after a wonderful time of fun and laughter with our brothers and sisters-in-law, I used their home landline to call my friend. I wanted to see if she had received my message and wanted to have lunch and meet my husband. It was as though not a day, month, or year had passed in our friendship! "Yes, Jo! I would love to see you and meet your husband! Why not come to my house and we'll visit a bit before lunch? I'm so excited to see you."

THERE IS NO TIME NOR SPACE BETWEEN FRIENDS

God had orchestrated that moment. I had tried for several years to reunite with my dear friend and now I can see it wasn't my timing, but His timing that was perfect. When we looked into each others faces, we saw no tired eyes, no wrinkles, no grey hair, no fears, doubts, or insecurities. We saw only the beautiful face of friendship, finally reunited with one another in this one amazing moment.

A few hours after lunch was cleared, Don excused himself to explore the area around the town and get some exercise. Of course, I knew he had intentionally left us alone to breathe in these precious moments of renewed friendship. We rolled out our canvas of hurt onto the table. Our former images of each other had become dull, cracked, and faded because our relationship had been stored in darkness and silence for so long. Confusion, sadness, judgment, disappointment, and misunderstanding covered our cloth. It took painful and honest sharing of our feelings, each listening carefully while confessing our weaknesses and shortcomings. Before long, we had used the palette knife of God's Grace to scrape the dirty, cracked paint off our old canvas and onto the floor to be remembered no more.

We forgave each other out of our love for Christ. The fabric of our friendship had always been strong, but it was in need of some R & R—repair and restoration! We had taken the first step of forgiveness. Hopefully, renewal would come with time.

A few more hugs, a few quick photographs to mark the day, and my friend and

I said our "good-byes-for-now." I drove home full of gratitude in my heart to God, thanking Him for the milestone day—His perfect timing and His perfect portrayal of friendship.

The face of friendship is painted with strokes of continued love, respect, loyalty, honesty, sacrifice, and devotion, mingled with bright colors of joy, laughter, celebration, silliness, and pure fun—all covered with a wash of God's blessings. For friends, indeed, are God's blessings in our lives.

HIS GRACE : THE VALUE OF FRIENDSHIP

Friendship with other women enlarges our hearts, making room for female interests, small talk and laughter, and sharing life together as friends, wives, and moms. As we mature, we become more aware of our choice of friends. Our friends reflect who we are, including shared values and the willingness to hold each other accountable as we grow in the Lord daily.

As iron sharpens iron, so one person sharpens another.

— Proverbs 27:17

Friends also help us grow and mature, discover who we are, and support us in our tender, hurtful spots. Friends bring richness and fullness to marriage and to motherhood. Being with true friends gives us a safe place to express our emotions, knowing they will listen with love, understanding, and empathy.

True friends will walk with us through the adventure of our calling—helping us discover our gifts and passions. I think of all the shared experiences through celebration—the beautiful weddings and baby showers, graduation celebrations, weddings, births, birthdays, and holiday celebrations. I also think of "celebrations of the heart," little milestones shared only with those you love, as well as shared difficulties. As we journey through life, may we remember those who have encouraged us spiritually.

Who has walked with you through the "aches" of motherhood? Through the mourning and loss of a parent, spouse, or child? Through rebuilding your life after the storm of divorce? Through the retooling of your life after you have lost everything? Who has walked with you through a long illness or a desert journey?

I love the Willow Tree Collection of figurines. I shared a very special keepsake with my two daughters, for they, indeed, are my authentic friends and precious treasures—three women, joined arm in arm and titled, "By My Side":

"From each other, over the years

we gather strength through laughter and tears."

TENDING OUR FRIENDSHIPS

Recalling the names of your friends from early childhood onward, I hope you see the steady stream of friends God has so lovingly sprinkled along your path, bringing a richness, flavor, and support to help with navigating your stones in the river. There have been times I've prayed for friends when I was lonely or isolated. There have been answers when God sent angels in the form of friends to minister to me in my grief.

Friends come in all shapes and sizes. We'll be disappointed if we try to label or characterize who we think should be our friends. Sometimes people seek us out for reasons of their own. They see in us something they find attractive, or we look easy to

approach. More importantly, God has sent them to us so they can receive what He wants us to give. If we turn away, He will find someone else to fill the void. So, I begin my day with, "Lord, I'm going to 'suit up and show up' and you send me the people you want to cross my path. I'll know they're from You!" If you do this, you'll never have a dull day, believe me! Be prepared for distractions and interruptions!

We do need discernment in our choice of friends. In the process of gathering friends with the same interests, common goals, and shared experiences, there may come a time of letting go. Not all friends are healthy for us. We need to ask God for wisdom and discernment in choosing our friends, being selective so as not to spread ourselves too thin.

I had a friend in college who had just been hired on as a bank teller. He shared how they were trained to spot counterfeit bills. They worked only with legal tender throughout the day. Now and then, their boss would hide a counterfeit bill in the pile. They could identify it immediately. I apply that knowledge to friendships. I prayed for my daughters to know true friendship early in their lives so that the counterfeits would be easy to spot!

Back-biting, gossip, and slander are not only destructive and degrading, but they also reflect back upon us. The person we're sharing with knows we will talk the same way about him or her when he or she is not in our presence. Without trust in our friendships, we are unable to truly share our deeper selves. Besides it is morally degrading to ourselves and to our relationship with the Lord. (Now I'll get off my soapbox, but see Proverbs 16:28, 17:9, 17:17, 18:24, 27:6, & 27:10.)

Put on then, as God's chosen ones, holy and beloved,

compassionate hearts, kindness, humility, meekness, and patience,

bearing with one another and, if one has a complaint against another,

forgiving each other, as the Lord has forgiven you,

so you also must forgive. And above all these, put on love,

which binds everything together in perfect harmony.

— Colossians 3:12-14

Often God will send someone we need in our life to shake us up or strengthen us for God's refinement and purpose. God placed women in my path when I was a younger mother and felt as though I was running 120 mph. These wise women slowed me down long enough to evaluate what was important, rather than urgent. I also had two women who were my spiritual mentors during my years of raising my daughters. I spent time with them in person and in notes, telling them how grateful I was to them for investing in me. Both live several hours away now, however, I visit when I can and make the most of the time I have with them. I'll share more later about the need for us to turn around and reach for the young women in our lives, being available to them in their womanhood and spiritual growth.

Molly, my spiritual mentor

Whether chairing women's retreats, working with ministry fundraising, raising money for the Girls Soccer League or Children's Hospital, or working for a common goal, the experiences we share with friends create an unforgettable bond. The act of giving unites us. People love to help where they feel they are needed. Social connection is critical to our health and wellbeing. Staying in touch requires time and attention but is so worthwhile. This is especially true in regard to social

My command is this: Love each other as I have loved you.

Greater love has no one than this:

that he lay down his life for his friends.

You are my friends if you do what I command.

I no longer call you servants,

because a servant does not know his master's business.

Instead, I have called you friends,

for everything that I learned from my Father

I have made known to you. You did not choose me, but I chose you

and appointed you to go and bear fruit—fruit that will last.

Then the Father will give you whatever you ask in my name.

This is my command: Love each other.

— *John* 15:12-17

media; we need to remember to physically fellowship together.

No matter where we gather as friends, the important thing to realize is that life is a journey, with heartache, pain, laughter, and joy. Our stories intertwine, joining us together forever. The beauty of time is that it never stands still. No matter where we are on this line of continuum from here to eternity, there are wonderful experiences waiting ahead for us.

HIS LOVE : JESUS CHRIST, OUR PERFECT FRIEND

Our primary relationship is with Jesus Christ, our Lord and Savior. He is our eternal friend, connected through the ultimate friendship—our friendship with the Father. God is our one true friend who will never let us down. Here on earth, true friendship is based on the love and commitment in our hearts to follow Christ. Choose your friends wisely, ensuring they are people who you want to emulate and who possess qualities of those who love our Lord. We, as well as our friends who share our love and commitment to Jesus as their Lord and Savior, will be together for all eternity! Jesus Christ modeled perfect friendship during His time on earth, so we could follow in His footsteps.

When the Pharisees got together, one of them,
an expert in the law, tested him with this question:
'Teacher, which is the greatest commandment in the Law?'
Jesus replied, 'Love the Lord your God with all your heart,
all your soul, and with all your mind.'
This is the first and greatest commandment.
And the second is like it: 'Love your neighbor as yourself.'

— Matthew 22:37

My sister Mary Jo and me

THE TRIPOD OF LIFE

There are three major supports in our lives. All of the supports are relational and all of them have been given to us by God. They are the three legs of a stool upon which we rest:

The first is our spiritual support, that genuine, intimate relationship with the Triune God—the Father, Jesus, His Son, and the Holy Spirit. It carries the greatest weight in our hearts.

The second is our family support, which, by God's design, is the very foundation of emotional and physical wellbeing. Our husband, sons, sons-in-law, grandsons, daughters, daughters-in-law, granddaughters, and beyond are all to be treasured, nurtured, respected, and honored.

The third is our friendship support, filling in the cracks and crevices mingled among our stones in the river, making our lives a heaven on earth. Some friends come into our lives for an hour, a day, a month, or a season.

The friendship stories I've shared here, as in the previous and still-to-come stones, are just some of the special women God has placed in my life—some for a reason, some for a season, some for forever—but all have left footprints on my heart and changed me forever.

The very nature of the stones we navigate throughout life allows for an overlay of the people and experiences that make us who we are today. So it was appropriate that my last year of BSF in Laguna Beach with my precious prayer sisters and friends was the study of Moses.

My friends and the Moses Study prepared me for my desert journey ahead.

"Some friends come into our lives for awhile
and quickly go. Some stay for awhile
and leave footprints on our hearts
and we are changed forever."

— *Anonymous*

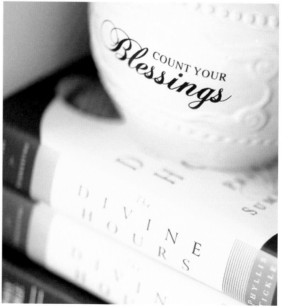

- Can you remember a time Jesus seemed to wait to answer your prayer? What did you learn about Him in that experience?

- Take the time to make a list of all your friends. List those whom you have maintained since childhood, high school, or college. What about those years when raising your family? Look for ways God has been faithful to you in the past, always sending friends to come along side you. To do life with you or fill in the gap. It will give you a look back at the tapestry God was weaving into your life.

- We give a great gift to our children by having the same friends throughout their lifetime.

- Friends bind us together as we navigate the stones of life, giving depth and dimension and beauty to our lives. Take good care of them; treasure them as gifts from God.

- Friends are irreplaceable. If they are healthy and affirming friends, send them a note or, better yet, pick up the phone and tell them how much you appreciate them.

- The best way to have a friend is to be a friend. A great common denominator is the bond of working together toward a common heartfelt goal. Some women are more suited to larger groups of friendships and others to smaller, more intimate groups, or even one on one. Which best describes you? Above all, be yourself, and don't judge others. Be authentic and true to yourself. There will be a countenance about you which draws others to you, seeking to know what's different about you. Life is an adventure when we plan our days, then step aside as He brings us His interruptions.

- I hope you have a close friend, "a friend who sticks closer than a brother" (Prov.18:24). A true, close, personal friendship is truly a great blessing. Read the story of Jonathan and David in your Bible, for one such story. 1 Samuel 1-15 in the Old Testament tells of their lasting legacy.

- Draw close to Jesus Christ, our Lord and precious Savior, your Perfect Friend, who is calling you to draw near to Him for intimacy and love.

Remember how the Lord your God
    led you all the way into the desert these forty years
        to humble you
        to test you in order
        to know your heart.

        — **Deuteronomy 8:2**

STONE 7   DESERT JOURNEYS

*N*ine o'clock on a Monday evening found me cuddled with a hot cup of chamomile tea as I read my real estate book, preparing for my upcoming state certification exam. I heard Don walk in the front door talking with our daughter and son-in-law. How strange, I thought. Shannon and I had worked together in the shop that day and had both said we looked forward to a quiet evening at home. As I got up to greet them all, I knew by the looks on their faces that this was not a normal visit.

Don asked me to sit down because he had some bad news. He explained that he had not wanted to alarm me when he discovered a plum-sized lump on the side of his throat while shaving several days earlier. A fellow physician had agreed it was, indeed, a tumor.

Assuming his role as professional physician, Don carefully laid out the care program the doctors recommended for him. It would begin three days later with surgery to take a biopsy and make a diagnosis. I tried my best to mask the panic I felt at such a sudden turn of events.

The next three days seemed like a hundred as we made plans for Don to place his medical practice on hold. A few close OB-GYN colleagues would take over the care and delivery of his female patients who were approaching their due dates. As we women know, changing physicians can be difficult and emotionally upsetting, especially in our last trimester! But it had to be done and his patients awaiting surgery had to be rescheduled.

"Hardships often prepare ordinary people for an extraordinary destiny."

— *CS Lewis*

With family and close friends, we prayed for good news—but his biopsy results were not good. My husband had a malignant tumor with stage III squamous cell carcinoma at the base of his tongue. They gave him a 3 to 4 months prognosis.

The doctor sat with us as they carefully laid out the care program, beginning with six weeks of daily radiation to shrink the tumor, followed by six rounds of chemotherapy to destroy the cancer cells. They would then perform a second radical surgery in hopes of an improved prognosis. Rods would be inserted beneath his chin, from one ear to the other, connecting directly with the tumor. He would receive continuous radiation for four days, twenty-four hours a day. Other than a nurse monitoring his morphine drip several times a day, he would be alone in the room. I would be allowed to visit for just ten minutes each morning while draped with a radiation shield. Our daughters would not be allowed in because they were child-bearing age.

HIS TESTING : I GO BEFORE YOU

Deserts, by nature, are dry, dusty, barren, perilous, and without visual borders. Deserts are hostile to life. Resources are scarce. Life in the desert is hard. Few of us choose to enter a desert, but sometimes the Lord calls us aside into one. We find ourselves experiencing a sudden pause in the harmony of our lives, squinting our eyes at life, trying to adjust to the unrecognizable topography.

That is where Don and I found ourselves as I turned the calendar to June 1st—Desert Day—knowing we were entering unchartered territory. I had just spent the previous nine months studying the life of Moses in BSF and realized that God had once again gone before me. The Lord had prepared our steps.

As I was with Moses, so I will be with you;
I will never leave you or forsake you.
Be strong and courageous."

— *Joshua 1:5-6*

God has given clear instruction about how to survive a desert journey. We are to stick close to the Lord, not be anxious to see too far ahead, nor fear the next step, nor be too eager to choose the path, nor be weighted down with heavy belongings. We are to have no fear of the future, but quietly follow behind The Shepherd, one step at a time. There is to be no murmuring or complaining, only obedience. We are to be dependent on God to sustain us daily in His Word as He provides the manna we need, one day at a time. So, into the desert we went, never dreaming this stone would require a seven-year journey.

HIS PROVISION : AN OASIS IN THE DESERT

We struggled as we adjusted to a new normal. With Don unable to practice medicine or deliver babies, another OB-GYN took on his busy practice in addition to his own. What a tremendous relief, allowing Don to recuperate and focus fully on his recovery. His surgery and direct radiation gave us all hope for remission, but it was impossible for Don to eat most foods due to the ulcerated sores in his mouth and throat. He suffered unrelenting fatigue and increasing loss of energy.

In the midst of all these challenges, we discovered the loss of income and piling debt made it impossible to keep our house. Having successfully passed my real estate exam, I gathered all my confidence and drove to the busiest Coldwell Banker realtor office in our area. Upon meeting with the newly assigned female manager, she told me that as a rule, they did not hire agents without experience. I pleaded my case. An hour later, I left the office with a new career start date!

God gave me that job!

Being employed with a broker office allowed me to sell our home myself, while being under the supervision of a top agent in the office. It also meant I would save the seller's agent commission!

I held our first open house the next Sunday while Meghan took Don to a movie for the afternoon. We had three offers the first day! My daughters and I packed up the house after finding another smaller house and praised God for His blessings.

But all would not go smoothly. It never does in the desert. The week after escrow closed, we were sued by the buyer for not disclosing a crack in the foundation of the living room floor. But I had disclosed it. I had taken back the carpet and shown her the crack, and I had also taken a photo of it for my own protection. When we had bought the house seven years previously, the previous owner had done the same. Because we had signed the Arbitration Clause in the closing escrow papers, our case would go before a judge in a closed meeting.

Once again, God had gone before us. Meghan had a great summer job with a top real estate attorney in our area who agreed to represent us. Don was too weak to leave the house or even speak at this time, so I went to the arbitration hearing by myself. I was definitely on my knees before God in preparation for the meeting. I was emotionally and physically exhausted, caring for Don around-the-clock while rummaging through all our files and photographs to ensure I had everything prepared. I felt a vise of fear tightening around me as I tried not to get ahead of the Lord.

The judge listened to both sides of the case. After both attorneys and the representing agent of the plaintiff had pleaded their cases, the judge asked everyone to leave the room except for me. He returned to the room and quietly took a seat beside me. With humility and kindness, he asked me what was going through my mind and if I wanted to add anything. God took over, as I shared from my heart!

With honesty and confidence, I relayed my belief that God was in control of the outcome of this decision. I found myself boldly telling him about my Moses study, how the Lord had prepared us for the difficult journey of my husband's illness and this lawsuit. I pleaded innocence to deceiving anyone. I told how I had asked the buyer to look under the carpet so she would know the crack existed, sharing that it had been there when we purchased the house. I compared the two pictures, showing the crack had not worsened over time. Finally I declared, "Whatever the outcome, we will be fine, because God is in control. I know He is faithful and just."

The judge then asked everyone to reconvene. Standing beside me, he stated that he, too, had prepared for this case. He had researched the buying history of the plaintiff and discovered that she and her real estate agent had two previous real estate transactions together. They had gone into litigation with the sellers and won both times—but he said, "Not this time!" He required the plaintiff pay all attorney fees and advised them he was reporting the sales agent to the California Real Estate Association to have her real estate license revoked, pending further charges!

"Case closed!"

As my attorney and I stayed behind to thank him, the judge wished us God's blessings on our desert journey and offered to be of help if ever we needed anything. He claimed that he, too, had experienced God's faithfulness and might in his own desert journey and sought every day to have His justice prevail.

Here was a fellow traveler who knew of God's faithfulness. As if to make his point, he simply pointed to his nameplate on the table: *Judge Abraham.*

And the Lord will continually guide you,
And satisfy your desire in scorched places,
And give you strength to your bones;
And you will be like a watered garden,
And like a spring of water whose waters do not fail.

— Isaiah 58:11

I praised God all the way home!

My job, the savings on our house sale, and now this judge being assigned to our case—all evidence of God's hand all around us providing and protecting His own as we navigated another stone in the river of God's faithfulness.

HIS STRENGTH : CAREGIVING

Caregiving is both a privilege and a challenge. It is a privilege to love and give all we have to those we love, yet it is also a tremendous physical challenge that tests our emotional endurance. I thought I was strong, but this was tough and strained me spiritually, as well. Don was bravely enduring a barbaric treatment. It broke my heart to see him in such discomfort and pain. The ulcerated sores in his mouth were aggravated by the tracheotomy they gave him to keep his airway clear. The visits with our homecare nurse encouraged and trained me in his care, but the sole responsibility I felt for his wellbeing was overwhelming.

Dear Reader, if you have served as a caregiver, you know of this lonely journey. One day, one week, one month, one year—the unrelenting responsibilities and demanding rigors of caregiving can wear us to the bone as we're stretched far beyond what we think we can do and be. I simply began to fall apart. Shannon and Steve had moved to Baltimore with our one-year-old grandson, while Meghan was in her junior year of college in San Francisco. My stepmom and sister were busy caring for my dad, who was in declining health. At times I struggled with fear, loneliness, and isolation. Our family and friends were answers to prayer when they would call or drop by with dinner and a surprise visit. My friends and prayer partners shared my burden, encouraged and loved us, and reminded us God was in control.

Thank goodness the washing machine and dryer were located in a secluded area of our garage. I kept a stepstool and box of Kleenex there for the times I needed to let go and plead to God for help. I would put in a load of clothes for sound protection and just cry, releasing guttural sounds so deep I didn't recognize myself. I begged God to take this cup from us, to restore Don to health, and to enable me to stay in good health to take care of him.

Jo, "gird yourself with strength." (Proverbs 31:17)

"Pick up your bootstraps, Sweetie, and keep going!"— My dad!

God reveals Himself to those He calls. He knows us and is concerned about us. He hears our groans and is faithful to keep His promises. Take a moment to reflect on God's faithfulness in the past. How has He prepared you for what you are experiencing now? By having to lean on God and God alone, I knew He was with me in the desert, teaching me patience and the hard emotional and physical labor of caregiving. He always gives us strength for the journey when we need it most.

God taught me and humbled me every day by that washer and dryer! He emptied me out so He could fill me up with all that was of Him. As Moses said, God brings us out to take us in (Deut. 6:23). Have you learned this invaluable lesson, dear one? Do not forget all the Lord has done for you. Do not fret. Do not forget God's goodness, faithfulness, and purpose for you and your life. He wants our wholehearted commitment. Nothing else will do. There are times in all our lives when we ask God, "Why me?!" But the more pertinent question is, "Why *not* me?" Why am I not a perfect candidate to learn obedience through suffering? What a gift!

When God asks us to wait upon Him, it takes great strength, discipline, and trust, but we need to do it. Then sit back and watch what happens. He will use our circumstances to teach us, train us, and grow us in full knowledge of Him.

BIBLE MARGIN: 1997

When things seem impossible, Jo, do not say, "Oh, Lord, what am I going to do?!" When things happen in my life that are not in my control, I need to wait (PATIENCE) and see what GOD has on the road ahead of me...so, instead, I need to ask, "Oh, Lord, what are YOU going to do?!"

BANKRUPT AND BROKEN

The desert looks different for each person, but it's always difficult. God didn't send his people of Israel the short, easy way home (Exodus 13:17). He sent them through the desert. God used that desert time to instruct and mature His people to follow Him. The easy road would have led them to disaster. God takes us the hard way for our good and His glory. He is faithful.

Don and I plodded on in our desert journey. We couldn't quit. There was no turning back, so we trudged forward.

We were thrilled when Meghan graduated from college and came home to work with us at the office. Don had recovered and grown strong enough to be driven to the office three days a week to see patients. It was the best medicine the doctor could have ordered! Before long, he was working full-time again and had returned to his surgery and delivery schedule, albeit abbreviated, with no night or weekend call. His medical colleague had proven to be a reliable, skilled, responsible partner, so he and Don joined offices and shared Don's patients. Praise God, he was in remission!

We enjoyed the oasis in the desert for two years. Soon the physical demands of his large practice became too much for him and Don had to face every doctor's dread— retirement. Don's incredible medical career included graduating from Stanford Undergraduate, Graduate, and Medical School, doing his Internship and Residency at

Stanford University Hospital, serving as a Captain in the US Army Medical, partnering with another physician in an OB-GYN medical practice for thirty-six years until his partner died suddenly of a brain aneurism. Don had delivered over 10,000 babies in his forty-four year medical career while serving on staff and Chair at three major hospitals. The doctors, nurses, and staffs at each of them held wonderful retirement parties for him. Our family and friends honored and celebrated him. Following retirement, he was able to do short-term locum tenancy assignments, filling in for other physicians when they were ill or on vacation. It was a welcome transition.

Don's remission continued for several months, when, unannounced, he began having TIAs (Transient Ischemic Attacks)—mini-strokes in the brain. They increased in strength with each occurrence. Within the year, they were occurring more frequently, making it more worrisome to be away from home. Daily life and caregiving went into crisis mode. In the midst of escalating stress and exhaustion, I could still feel the prayers of my family and friends. However, when I was alone at the end of each day, panic and fear crept into our house. God was going to have His way with me: "Stand still. Sit still. Be still, Jo. I have things to teach you."

As we were driving to his doctor's appointment one morning, Don suffered a serious attack. I drove him straight to the hospital, gripping the steering wheel with white knuckles and praying for God's strength for both of us. This one had done some damage. He spent three days in the hospital before they transferred him to a rehabilitation facility for another three weeks.

Three weeks later, he was ready to leave rehab but not ready for home. The physicians determined he would need full-time nursing care for at least two months to allow him to regain body strength and mental skills for eating and self-care. We found a lovely facility close to home. After a tour and meeting the staff, the director said it would be best if I went on home while they got Don settled into his new environment.

I cried all the way home, the image of him shuffling along, leaning on his nurse, replayed over and over in my mind's eye. Though he had smiled as I left, I knew it was going to be a long two months for both of us.

With Don settled into the fully- staffed care facility, my boss recommended I take a small break for myself to prepare for all the changes in the next phase of caregiving. Our home needed to be retrofitted for handicapped requirements, but once that was completed, and with Don's blessing, I headed south to a Spiritual Retreat.

It was a silent retreat, with evenings for dinner and fellowship where I met so many wonderful women. The time away was restful—reading God's Word, prayer journaling, and taking plenty of outdoor walks.

> *Taken aside by Jesus, to feel the touch of His hand.*
> *To rest for awhile in the shadow of the Rock in a weary land.*
> *Taken aside by Jesus, in the loneliness, dark and drear,*
> *Where no other comfort may reach me,*
> *Than His voice to my heart so dear.*
> *Taken aside by Jesus to be quite alone with Him,*
> *To hear His wonderful tones of love,*
> *'Mid the silence and shadows dim.*
> *Taken aside by Jesus, shall I shrink from this desert place,*
> *When I hear as I never heard before,*
> *And see Him face to face.*

> *— Streams in the Desert, August 27*

Jesus was most precious to my soul in quiet, prayerful times as I confessed to Him I was a broken vessel. I was at the end of myself. I begged Him to help me. I became aware of the unresolved emotions inside with which I hadn't yet dealt. They were demanding and severe, now pouring forth like hot lava onto a beautiful Mauna Kea beach. Pain. Sadness. Sorrow. Anger. Resentment. Fear. Abandonment.

The last morning of the retreat, we were invited to write these down and nail them to the cross. I begged God to cleanse my heart of everything that was not of Him and bury it deep in the graveyard of sin. The Lord took it all and buried it deep.

Refreshed and renewed with God's touch, I gave it all to Him and returned home, ready for the path the Lord had set before us. Don was working hard and making new friends and acquaintances. He was kept busy all day until we enjoyed long visits together in the evening.

THE BLESSING IN THE LIBRARY

The night before he was to be discharged for home, a close group of friends planned something special. They wanted to pray over Don and anoint him with healing oil. They settled Don into a wingback chair in a quiet corner of the library. Don was enveloped and surrounded with love and prayers from these Godly men that night. They stormed the Throne of Grace for Don, begging God's favor upon him, asking for God to give His healing touch and surround him with His peace and comfort. They asked that Don would know his salvation was secure.

God touched Don that evening. The next morning he shared his experience with me: "I met God last night. All I want to do, from today forward, is to use every day of life He gives me to love, praise, and serve Him." The sweetest flowers grow deep in the canyons of life. There are lessons that can only be learned in the valley with our Savior Lord. We praised God for choosing us for this journey, for being our Strength, our Hope, and our Courage. Most of all, we praised God for His faithfulness, for though we were still unsure of where His path was leading, we could feel our weights becoming wings.

"We look at our burdens and heavy loads,

and shrink from them; but as we lift them

and bind them about our hearts, they become wings,

and on them we rise and soar toward God."

There is no burden which, if we lift it cheerfully

and bear it with love in our hearts,

will not become a blessing to us.

God means our tasks to be our helpers;

to refuse to bend our shoulders to receive His

load is to decline a new opportunity for growth."

—J. R. Miller

Don was frail and fragile, but wanted to help me in any way he could so as not to be a burden. I had stayed up late one night addressing our Christmas card envelopes. The cards themselves were scheduled to be ready the next day. I wanted to have everything stamped and ready to simply stuff the envelopes and drop them in the mail. I finished addressing the envelopes, applied the adhesive return address labels, and affixed all the stamps. I neatly sorted them into two piles—one for in-town and one for out-of-town mailing. Exhausted, I fell into bed at 2:30 am, happy to have everything ready to go.

On my way home from work the next day, I picked up the imprinted cards. Following dinner, I eagerly sat down to add a short note to each card, especially for out-of-town friends.

"Honey, where are all those envelopes I had sitting on the table?" I called.

"Oh, Richard took me for lunch, so I sealed all the envelopes for you and dropped

Bless the Lord, O my soul;

And all that is within me, bless His Holy Name.

Bless the Lord, O my soul,

And forget none of His benefits;

Who heals all your diseases,

Who redeems your life from the pit;

Who crowns you with loving kindness and compassion;

Who satisfies your years with good things,

So that your youth is renewed like the Eagle. . .

. . . For as high as the heavens are above the earth,

So great is His loving kindness toward Those who fear Him.

As far as the East is from the West,

So far has He removed our transgressions from us.

— Psalm 103:1-5, 11-12

them off at the post office so they could go out today! I wanted to surprise you!"

I resisted my impulse to have a meltdown and replied, "Well, yes, it will be quite a surprise for everyone to receive an empty envelope for their Christmas greeting!"

And that is how a hidden blessing arrived. At least half of our friends who received those stamped, empty, sealed envelopes called us to report the mystery of the missing card. Since I was often at work, Don had a good laugh reconnecting with old friends who called about what had happened. More importantly, he was encouraged and blessed by each person who called. Some blessings come to us quietly in the desert, unrecognized until a later time. Isn't it beautiful how the Lord works? He is the God of every detail.

BLESSINGS ALONG THE WAY

It was seven years after the cancer diagnosis—and, oh, what blessings God had given us along the way. Family and friends continued to lighten our burden. We shared every milestone together and continued to enjoy celebrations through the pain:

- Meghan graduated college
- I became a Coldwell Banker Real Estate Sales Agent
- 2nd Grandson, Zackary born (1996)
- Meghan and Brandon married (1998)

- Four granddaughters, two from each daughter and son-in-law, born in just 27 months! (1999-2001)—Payton, Madeline, Quinn, Catherine
- 7th Grandchild, Abigail born (2002)
- Marriott Newport Coast Villas, sales agent, surrounded by strong leadership, training, and friendships (saved our financial lives!)

Even when life is hard, how God must love it when we lift our arms to heaven and offer Him a brave and thankful heart.

HIS WILL : OUR GARDEN OF GETHSEMANE

As we were driving one beautiful, sunny day, Don pointed out an enormous, fluffy, white cloud, hovering between two mountainsides, heading to the oceans edge. "Honey, look at that beautiful cloud. I see it there most days from our living room window about this time." After a thoughtful pause, he continued. "When you see that cloud, Jo, I want you to take heart and remember how much I love you, now and forever."

He could see I was swallowing back tears. "When I'm no longer here with you," he whispered, "I want you to be strong. Be strong and courageous, Honey. You needn't be afraid, because you know I will be with the Lord. You can rely on the Lord's presence and comfort with you. Will you promise me you'll do that?"

Two months later, calls were made to our family to come to the hospital. Don's daughter, son, daughter-in-law, and two daughters arrived from the east coast. Steve and Shannon and their four young children came from Atlanta, and Brandon and Meghan and their two daughters all came quickly.

Don had fallen with a severe TIA one morning while we were having morning coffee. He never spoke after his surgery. After everyone had arrived, we all circled around his bed to sing songs the children knew—"Jesus Loves Me," "This Little Light of Mine," and

Father, if Thou art willing,
    remove this cup from me,
yet not my will,
    but Thine be done.

— *Luke 22:42*

others. I was holding our little grandson, Zackary, when he looked down upon his bed. "Papa, look at you! You have no wrinkles!"

The next morning, his nurse, Grace, bathed him, anointed him with oil, and replaced the hospital gown with fresh, blue pajamas I had brought for him from home—ocean blue. She had placed white, fluffy pillows all around him for comfort. As I looked at his frail body through the tears, I was reminded of blue sky and the giant, white cloud Don had pointed out for me. I remembered the promise I had made to trust God through the storm that was about to come. As I held Don's hand, I leaned in to God's faithfulness.

One of life's greatest pains—and privileges—is to walk with someone we love to the threshold of death—that moment when their soul leaves their physical body and takes flight to Heaven with Jesus. No matter how long it takes, we are never ready. The journey together ends all too quickly.

I had kept my Bible close while staying day and night with Don in the hospital, making notes in the margin of the last five days of our journey together. The evening of his passing, my Bible was bookmarked on this Psalm. It was like a final kiss.

Wait for the Lord;
Be strong, and let your heart take courage;
Yes, wait for the Lord.

—Psalm 27:14

The desert looks different for each and every person. This season of life was my journey; yours will be different, but deserts will come. Take heart, my friend. It is only for a season. God will use it to accomplish His work within you. A desert journey brings us to the end of ourselves, emptying our self-reliant hearts and refilling us with God's truths and His immeasurable gifts of comfort and grace.

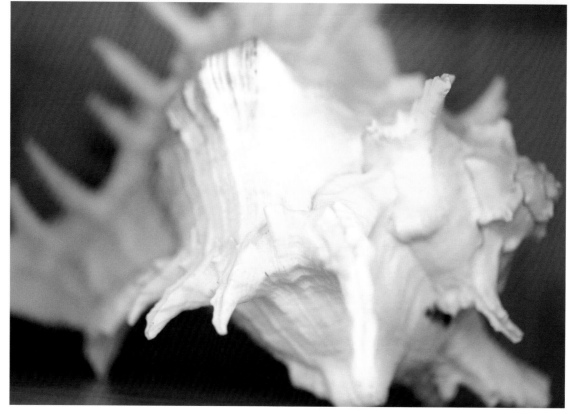

GRACE NOTES | *Desert Journeys*

- In what ways has God called you aside, into the dry desert? Perhaps you are enduring financial trials or separation from family or loved ones, hardships, pain, suffering, loss, or several combined! Trust Him. He will never leave you or forsake you.

- We would all like to imagine we would be ready if a crisis suddenly occurred in our lives, but, if truth be known, a crisis only reveals the lack of preparedness within us. Often instead of being found ready for battle, we would be revealed as unfit. Once the crisis has come, it is too late to begin to fortify and fill our crisis account. Treasure your time in prayer to be prepared when challenges arise.

- We all know life can change on a dime. The first blush of crisis is only the introduction to unchartered territory. Stick close to the Lord and welcome the support lines He gives you of family and friends. Lean into the Lord. Go to Him with your needs, pour out your heart. He will be there, speaking words of comfort and hope as you travail the thorny path.

- Perhaps you find yourself in a desert journey now. God is with you. Reflect on how He has prepared you for what you are experiencing now.

- Dear Reader, even the most faithful have doubt at times in their walk with the Lord, especially during tough times. As the saying goes, "If God feels far away, guess who moved?" Draw near to Him. Read His Word in the Bible, asking the Holy Spirit to prepare your heart to hear His Word, His love letter to you. Every answer to life is found in His Word.

- Weakness in prayer precedes weakness in battle. In battle, the slow and the stragglers are always in the back of the army, where they can be attacked.

- Other than my own church community, I would tell you the three greatest impacts on my spiritual life were; God's gifts of the friendships and teaching of Bible Study Fellowship, the friendships of my mentors and prayer partners which grew from that fellowship, placing me with equally yolked, same minded committed Christian women, and the three-year study of the Master's Program for Women, women who fed my soul.

The Lord is near to the brokenhearted,
And saves those who are crushed in spirit.

— *Psalm* 34:18

STONE 8   GRIEF AND LOSS

*L*oss. It's a season of life we all experience at some point in our journey. It's the tearing apart of someone or something we once thought secure. When we're deprived of someone we love, this stone of Grief and Loss can seem impossible to navigate.

No woman chooses to become a widow. Nothing can prepare her for it. We considered ourselves fortunate to have enjoyed Don for seven years beyond his diagnosis. It was a long good-bye, full of peaks and valleys, laughter and tears. Even so, I was in denial when he passed. I still believed he would be with us much longer. I wasn't emotionally prepared for the free-fall into grief.

I spent a few weeks after Don's passing with my family in Atlanta. Sorrow emptied my home while I was away. Don's absence left the rooms desolate and quiet, void of his voice, his shuffle, his loud television, his music, his painting... him. When I returned, his footprint was still everywhere. I listened to our voicemail recording several times a day just to hear his voice. I continually prayed, "Oh, dear Lord, please prepare me to endure this painful journey."

I clung to my 6:00 am quiet time with the Lord, coffee and candle by my side. I poured out my heart to the Lord, scribbling prayers in the margins of my Bible. Shannon faithfully called at 7:00, morning after morning, just to see how I was doing. My neighbor, Lisa, brought me a daily morning café latte along with her smile and encouragement. Meghan faithfully came by later on, kids in tow, big smiles on their

faces, eagerly hatching plans for the day. I spent countless evenings having dinner or talking on the phone with my stepmom or sister. Each of these moments was like a life preserver being thrown to me. I needed all these loved ones around me, reassuring me and giving their loving hugs! I couldn't verbalize it, but oh, how I missed physical touch.

I can't tell you how many times I thanked God for calling me closer to Him in my BSF study over those nine years, with the last year of Moses just eight years before. The greatest preparation for any curve ball in life is our intimate relationship with Christ and our life of prayer. My prayer sister, Donna, sent me this timely reminder in the mail shortly after Don passed away:

> *In Corrie ten Boom's book,* **The Hiding Place,** *Corrie was overwhelmed with the idea of ever losing a loved one. Her father reminded her of their trips to Amsterdam, and how he always gave her ticket to her just before they boarded the train. Her father told her that God does the same for us when a loved one dies, giving us the strength we need, just in time. There is no need to run ahead. God is there, lovingly preparing the way. God knows what we need and is faithful to provide just enough, just in time.*
>
> *— The Upper Room (Tuesday, April 23, 2002)*

HIS PROMISES : ALONE AT YOUR JORDAN

After a loss, after the flurry of family, friends, phone calls, and dinners, we see the rest of the world going on around us and realize our own life has come to a standstill. My world looked different now. The road was alien, crooked, with no familiar signposts.

Existing alone in this foreign place caught me off balance. Unable to find stable footing, I was disoriented and confused. I couldn't concentrate. I was forgetful and easily distracted, finding my mind had stopped listening to the world around me. At times I felt my grief subsiding, only to have it suddenly rear its intrusive head in the middle of a sentence. On occasion, the tears would flow when friends would ask how I was doing, even in the middle of the grocery store. They were so good to me; they never minded. I too have always thought it a tremendous privilege to have a friend or stranger cry in my presence.

They reminded me of a story I heard told by Christian radio host Paul Harvey.

When a little girl came home late, her mother scolded her for not returning when told. Her daughter replied, "Oh, Mommy, I couldn't leave my friend all by herself, because her dolly was broken."

"Well, honey," her Mommy asked, "what could you do to fix it?"

"Nothing. I just sat on the curb and cried with her."

I tried to think of friends who had walked this road before me, friends I could call on to sit on the curb with me, but I was the first one in our group of friends to lose a spouse. It was then the Lord seemed to whisper, "Jo, do not go to others. I am here. Come to Me for help."

Do not anxiously look about you, for I am your God.
I will strengthen you, surely, I will help you.
Surely I will uphold you with my righteous right hand.

— Isaiah 41:10

Do not fear, for I have redeemed you;
I have called you by name; you are Mine!
When you pass through the waters, I will be with you;
and through the rivers, they will not overflow you.
When you walk through the fire, you will not be scorched,
nor will the flame burn you; for I am the Lord your God,
the Holy One of Israel, your Savior.

Do not fear, for I am with you.

— Isaiah 41:1-3, 5

What do we do with our grief? What do we do while we march in place without moving forward? What do we do while awaiting God's guidance?

As the first of my friends to undertake this journey, it wasn't long before I discovered it is a solitary journey each of us must make on our own. We cannot go around the mountain; we have to go through it. No one can do the hard work of grief for us, but we do have the Holy Spirit with us to give comfort and courage. It is a path one must follow step-by-step, alone with the Lord, allowing the Holy Spirit to have His way with us while creating deep furrows in our soul. When learning simply to exist in the eye of the storm of grief, the term "dark night of the soul" is not too strong.

Jordan is the type of separation where there is no fellowship with anyone else, and where no one can take responsibility for you. You have to put to the test now what you learned when you were with Elijah. You have been to the Jordan over and over with Elijah, and now you are up against it alone. It is no use saying you cannot go; this experience has come, and you must go. If you want to know whether God is the God you have faith to believe Him to be, then go through your Jordan alone.

...At your Bethel you will find yourself at your wits' end and at the beginning of God's wisdom. When you get to your wits' end and feel inclined to panic, don't; stand true to God and He will bring His Truth out in a way that will make your life a sacrament.

— My Utmost for His Highest, August 11

I believed God was Who He said He was. I knew He was faithful. I knew He was my refuge, my strength, and my hope. I wanted to have Him make my life a sacrament, to be a visible sign of inward and spiritual grace, given in love from a loving and merciful Father. I knew from my readings that I could come out of this grief either bitter or better.

I chose better! I pointed my soul in one direction—towards the Lord—and kept it there.

BIBLE MARGIN: 2002

Jo, you are in a time of sadness and suffering, so TRUST GOD! When we go through grief, we either come out bitter or better! Well, there's no question what I'll do. I'm definitely going to come out of this better with Your help, Lord!

My Dear Reader, I share the journal entry below for a special reason. Some of you may need a life rope right now. You may be so lost in the depths of grief that you can't see your way out. I want to tell you as gently as I can what I have learned about loss: there is no way out—only through. Not to go through is to miss the blessing. The day of the following journal entry, I was where you are now. The Holy Spirit nudged me to see our pastor, the one who presided over Don's memorial service and the men's group which Don had attended weekly.

JOURNAL ENTRY: June 4, 2002

"Today I visited Pastor Pete. He helped me to see God's Plan... the BIG Picture... to keep my grief of losing Don SECOND to my love for the Lord. Pastor challenged me to 'remember to remember': Don is more than okay. He is with with Jesus in Heaven. I can always summon his memory; I can always have him close.

God loves me just the way I am, grieving mess and all! God comforts me and understands my sorrow in the grief of giving Don up to Him.

…And God asks, "Will you praise Me, Jo, even if I take Don away from you?"

"Yes, Lord! I will praise you in all circumstances."

In all these things we are more than conquerors through Him that loved us.

— Romans 8:37

Dear Reader, I pray that you too will "remember to remember." In your time of grief, God is also asking you, "Will you love Me and trust Me no matter what I send you?" The race of life only ends when we are in eternity with Christ. Becoming conquerors through Him that loved us (Romans 8:37) can only happen through journeys of struggle and crisis. My desert journey (1995-2002) flowed into my journey of loss and grief (2002-2005). I could not have made it through the storm without my sovereign God.

I continued to march in place, while actively seeking God's strength and direction each day. I waited in *prayer,* earnestly laying my grief at His feet. I waited in *patience,* knowing God was with me, giving me a peace in the waiting, being patient with myself as well. I waited in *faith,* seeking God's Word each morning.

THE SMALL COMFORTS

The firsts of everything are difficult when you've lost someone beloved: the first birthday, the first anniversary, the first Mother's Day, Father's Day, Easter, Thanksgiving, and Christmas. We found it best to create new traditions with each special occasion or to travel all together as a family to make new memories. Having the grandchildren around filled the days with laughter, joy, and celebration.

Show me Your ways,
O Lord; teach me Your paths.
Lead me in Your truth and teach me,
for You are the God of my salvation;
on You I wait all the day.

— Psalm 25:4

Yet Meghan and Brandon yearned for a new chapter and fresh challenge in their young lives. Brandon was cultivating an entrepreneurial adventure that needed to be planted in open spaces where it could bloom and grow and California did not meet those business criteria. Because Meghan was carrying their third baby, due in December, they decided to make their move to Coeur d'Alene, Idaho in early August. Steve and Shannon, and grandchildren were already in Atlanta, and now the thought of no longer having Brandon, Meghan, and granddaughters, right on the heels of losing Don felt like God was taking away all the underpinnings of my life.

I spent as much time as possible enjoying time with my granddaughters. Time waits for no one, however. Six weeks later I stood brokenhearted in the alley behind my house, holding back tears as my precious granddaughters drove off with their parents on their new journey. They waved madly from the back of the car, big smiles on their faces, yelling excitedly, "Bye, Grammie! See you soon! We love you, Grammie! See you in Idaho-ho-ho! We love you!"

I waved back just as madly, yelling, "I love you, too, my precious ones! See you soon! I love you!" I threw kisses until they were out of sight.

And then the circus tent collapsed. The extreme pain of my loneliness is hard to describe, but many of you are acquainted with such good-byes. A friend shared this portion of a poem with me:

"You expect this, when your children leave home....
Who would know that it hurts worse
To let go of a granddaughter...".

—*"Sadnest" by Cynthia Bates*

"He never promised you

an easy passage,

only a safe landing."

— *Streams in the Desert,*
March 31

Meghan and I spoke frequently; she was quite sensitive to what I was going through. Updates on her pregnancy, the house they were leasing, the weather, and what was going on with the girls all helped distract me, albeit briefly. I was counting the days until Christmas, when we'd be reunited.

I marked time with work. My real estate career was a lifesaver, both financially and emotionally. It was a focused, demanding position with the added benefit of wonderful friendships, all of which helped the time between August and December pass relatively quickly. I soon reunited with Shannon's family in Atlanta for Thanksgiving and with Meghan's family for Christmas in Coeur d'Alene.

One mid-December evening, my neighbor Lisa appeared at my door with a Christmas tree, all decorated with little white lights! We laughed as we hauled it into the living room and set it in the tree stand.

It was beautiful, simply beautiful!

She brought two new ornaments to hang on the tree, as well. One was a lovely glass angel. The other was a ceramic doghouse with a bone attached. On it she had written the name of my Golden Retriever, Amazing Grace. We laughed as we placed them on the tree, then we hugged each other and cried!

I left the tree as it was so lovingly offered to us, just me and my dog. It was more than enough. That season, I received priceless gifts from my Heavenly Father: simple, caring friendship and loving, abiding family, all wrapped in God's love. I heard Him whisper to my heart, "Merry Christmas, Jo."

Storms of bereavement are keen; but then, they are one of the Father's ways of driving me to Himself, that in the secret of His presence His voice may speak to my heart, soft and low.

— Streams in the Desert

HIS SHIELD : LIVING WITH GRIEF

I love to write in the margins of my Bible as I study God's Word. It's a way to share my heart with the Lord and see my spiritual progress later down the road. During my seven-year desert journey, I spent many, many hours with the Lord. It just happened (thanks to God's providence) that I had bought a new Bible without notes, praying for the Holy Spirit to lead and guide me through His Word, teaching me what He wanted me to learn. Although it was a word-for-word translation, I called it my "Living Bible" because the good, bad, and ugly of my days were splashed all over the margins of that Bible! I poured out my heart to the Lord on every page! I journaled in the margins of my daily devotionals, as well. Many of those notes are referenced in this book.

There are times and places where God will form a mysterious wall around us, and cut away all the props, and all the ordinary ways of doing things, and shut us up to something Divine, which is utterly new and unexpected, something that old circumstances do not fit into, where we do not know just what will happen, where God is cutting the cloth of our lives into a different pattern, where He makes us look to Himself.

— Streams in the Desert, April 5

GROWING IN FAITH THROUGH TEARS

I was blessed to have family and friends not only to encourage me, but also to serve as a barometer of how I was doing. The second year after losing Don was far more difficult than the first. The first year I merely limped along to keep going. The second year brought the profound realization that my life was never going to be the same again. One summer morning, both my girls and I were at the breakfast table talking after the kids had all run outside to play. They suggested that I might try a second grief group.

"Why?" I asked. "I think I'm doing so much better!"

"Actually Mom," my firstborn replied, "we think you would really benefit from another class now that life has settled down a bit. We're worried about you." I knew my daughters could see things I couldn't see, so I promised I'd look into it.

My second class was far more restorative than the first, I think, simply because I was now ready to do the real work of grief. I sat through the first three sessions just listening and feeling compassion for the others as they shared their loss. Near the end of our third session, the teacher asked if I would like to share. Though I had already shared the loss of my husband in an earlier class, I struggled to keep my composure. When I could finally trust my voice, I said, "Along with the grief of losing my husband, I find that I've lost me! I miss the Jo I used to know. I miss her laugh, her joy, her love, her caring. I want her back; my family wants her back!"

Our facilitator knew just what I meant. She had lost a daughter several years earlier and brought incredible insight and richness to us all. She looked at me and then to the other class members, pausing for several seconds before she tenderly answered, "I hate to tell you this, but the 'Jo' you knew is never coming back."

I cried all the way home! Running upstairs to my bedroom, I threw off my coat in preparation for throwing myself on my bed. I took off my high heels, one at a time, and threw them as hard as I could across the room, crying out to God to please help me! I had lost Don; I didn't want to lose me, too.

I looked across the room and saw shards of glass on the floor. One of my shoes had struck the glass shade of my favorite antique lamp with little children dancing

I can do all things through Christ,
Who strengthens me.

— *Philippians 4:13*

around the base. Well, I thought, isn't that just what I deserve for my outburst!

As I carefully gathered all the pieces of shattered glass into my hands, I looked down and remembered this quote from Henry Nouwen:

> *He chooses us.*
>
> *He blesses us.*
>
> *He breaks us.*
>
> *He shares us.*

I saved those glass shards in a little plastic bag in my drawer for some time. The lamp still sits on a dresser in my home. I love it even more with the big round hole in the top.

> *If through a broken heart God can bring His purposes to pass in the world, then thank Him for breaking your heart.*

> *— My Utmost for His Highest, November 1*

HIS MERCY : FINDING HOPE AGAIN

Somewhere in the second year after losing Don, I realized I had a decision to make: I could either continue looking in the rear-view mirror, living in my memories of the past, being haunted by *what-ifs*, feeling burdened and heavy-laden; or I could decide to cross the threshold and join the living again!

As I stood at the edge of that decision, I felt as Joshua must have felt when he had lost Moses. The desert was behind me, the Promised Land ahead, and the Lord was beckoning: "Come, Jo. I know it's unknown to you. *Trust Me.* I am with you. Seek Me only." God held out His Hand to me, and I reached for it.

I realized that I had been trying to make it on my own. I turned from my own way and said, "Yes!" to Jesus and "Yes!" to His plan for my life. I crossed the threshold by faith, trusting God instead of myself. I immersed myself in the Lord. I opened my heart to Him as never before, seeking Him morning and evening.

Once again, God proved to me that He is so faithful.

Slowly, God began to ignite the embers of hope within me.

The Lord provided His Word. I studied His Word while staying in prayer, keeping God's will for my life in the forefront. I tuned my heart to listen to His voice and let Him lead and guide me. I prayed to use my time wisely and learn well the lessons He had prepared for me. My deepest desire was to diligently seek Him, love Him, and serve Him with all my heart.

He sent me spiritual mentors, who helped me remember that God had a future purpose and plan for my life. They reminded me of Christ's promises to heal my broken heart. They helped me find strength for reaching out to others and trust God still had something new for me. They pushed me to grow in faith, courage, and trust in the Lord. I spent time with these dear ladies in a three-year Master's Program for Women, preparing us for our next life season. The program helped us identify our strengths and talents to make a significant impact in God's Kingdom, to prepare us to give to others that which the Lord had given to us. (I'll tell more of that in the next Stone!)

And most of all, God surrounded me through it all with loving family and faithful friends. Blessings are easy to overlook in grief, but we must not miss them! God sprinkles them along the paths of hard times with His encouragement: *Come on, keep going, I am with you!*

The journey through loss and grief is a slow and solitary journey. Traversing those deep furrows of our soul does bring us, at last, to the fresh, healing, living waters of our Savior, Jesus Christ. After we weather the storm, we will have a sharper sense of who we are in Christ, what is important to us, and what God's will is for the rest of our life.

And so I placed my toe in the water and left the banks of the Jordan and set my sights on all of the tomorrows the Lord had planned for me, thanking Him for blessing me with a love great enough to grieve so deeply and for precious relationships to pour into with all the love and grace God had shown me.

The Lord calls each of us out of the desert, eventually, into new life for His work. I left my desert of loss and grief eager to discover what the Lord had for me to do in the next season of life.

As I was with Moses, so I will be with you;
I will never leave you nor forsake you...
Be strong and very courageous.
Be careful to obey all the law my servant Moses gave you;
do not turn from it to the right or to the left,
that you may be successful wherever you go.
Do not let this Book of the Law depart from your mouth;
meditate on it day and night,
so that you may be careful to do everything written in it.
Then you will be prosperous and successful.
Have I not commanded you? Be strong and courageous.
Do not be terrified; do not be discouraged,
for the Lord your God will be with you wherever you go.

— Joshua 1:5-9

For Music Puccini
For Art Bernini For
Espresso Pasquini

For Music Puccini
For Art Bernini For
Espresso Pasquini

GRACE NOTES | *Grief and Loss*

- We never know when is "the last of the last": the last time together as a family, the last Christmas, the last fishing trip, the last time they say "I love you." Be mindful of the possibility that you may not have words of good-bye for those you love. Keep short accounts of your sin and anger. Seek or ask forgiveness as soon as you feel the nudge! Make amends as quickly as possible. "Blessed are the Peacemakers" (Matthew 5:9).

- After the lasts, the "firsts of everything" are difficult: the first time you come home to an empty house, the first time you go to church alone and come home alone, the first birthday. Give yourself time.

- Cry, play your music, read old letters, be alone or with family, talk it out; let grief have its way with you.

- God is our Redeemer. He will not waste our pain. Let His love wash over you and hear His voice.

- The storm of grief is fierce, but God uses it to call us unto Himself, that He may whisper to our hearts. Take your burden and lay it at His feet and *leave it there.*

- By facing our own suffering and grief, we will one day be able to truly help another soul facing loss and pain. Christ Himself suffered and was tempted in "all things" so we would know He truly understands our pain.

- It's good that we can't see the future. God gives us today: "Rejoice and be glad in it."

- There is joy in every Stone we encounter on the journey. Our sorrows will be made bright by the joys God plants all around us. Look for the "Blessings Along the Way."

- If during this season, God gives you the blessings of grandchildren, sing a song with them, rejoicing that your story will go on! Our children and grandchildren give us hope!

- As believers, remember that grief is not forever. We find healing through the deliberate, personal touch of the unfailing grace of God.

- Be forgiving of others, especially your family, who will think you are taking far too long to get on with your life! Be kind and listen to their concerns. Be grateful you are loved!

- Journal, journal, journal!

- One day you will find you have more good days than bad. Your healing has begun. Faith then becomes the harmony of our life.

Do not be anxious about anything,
but in everything, by prayer and petition,
with thanksgiving, present your requests to God.
And the peace of God,
which transcends all understanding,
will guard your hearts and minds in Christ Jesus.

— *Philippians 4:6-7*

STONE 9   SURRENDER AND RENEWAL

*W*hat's next, Lord? With determination and tenacity, I had been clinging to my Lord and Savior for nine long years, even when Satan told me my life looked hopeless. I was adapting to my children and grandchildren being far away and feeling so grateful we were together several times a year. I continued working long hours to keep up with the competitive real estate environment and my promotion to Team Leader.

Intent on putting aside as much money as possible into my retirement portfolio, I began working six days a week, sometimes for fourteen hours a day to stay on top of the bonus pool. It was not unusual for me to catch a flight after a work day to Idaho or Atlanta to see a grandchild's special event, then fly home the next day to report to work the next day at 8:00 am. I felt blessed to be with such an incredible company, to have incredible work associates, and enjoy great training. I thanked the Lord each morning in my quiet time, seeking only to do His will with each person He sent to me every day.

EMPTY YOUR VESSEL AND I WILL FILL IT

Grief no longer had the upper hand. There finally came a point where I was having more good days than bad days. With God's help, I was able to remember only the "glad days." I did my best to discipline my mind to focus on all the good times, to let go of the pain and store only the blessings of the past. When we express gratitude

"True faith drops its letter in the post office box and lets it go."

— *Streams in the Desert,*
April 24

and praise to the Lord for all He has given us, we open our hands and hearts to be filled with more blessings. Before we find our vessels empty, He has already refilled them. It is the Law of Divine Supply. He is our all; we need ask no other help!

One particular sunrise, I sat by the fireplace in my "prayer chair" with a hot cup of coffee and my Bible on my lap when I was startled by an unmistakable message:

"Jo, I have set you apart. I know your needs, for I am He who prepared your way. Trust in Me."

A SPIRITUAL MARKER : TRAINING OF THE MASTER

As I mentioned in the last Stone, I had begun my three-year study of The Master's Program for Women. I was successful in my Marriott career, but I had a deep yearning to do something significant for God's Kingdom. And I knew He had placed that desire upon my heart. It was my third year of widowhood.

I had been in deep, serious, urgent prayer since beginning The Master's Program nine months earlier. Suddenly, I had a realization: my ladder was leaning against the wrong building! I had been successful, but I really wanted to do what the Lord had prepared me to do these past seven years—whatever that was to be. I had an overwhelming and urgent need to know His calling for the second half of my life. It was as though, all of a sudden, I could see the evolution of His blessing: God had given me Marriott with my loving, supportive friends, and hard, stressful, rewarding work that helped keep my mind occupied during the sorrow and grief of losing Don. I had met such wonderful people in the marketplace, and it had saved our financial future.

Could God be calling me now to give up all of these "securities" He had blessed me with in order to gain freedom to start a new chapter with even more blessings?

When I came face to face with this question, I lost my passion at work. I knew more than ever that my position at work did not define me. Christ did. I knew My Master well enough to know He was getting ready to move me in His direction. This was between God and me. The more I pondered this, the more I felt Him pressing in upon me. I couldn't escape the question. The Hound of Heaven was once again on my tracks! Once we are in His grip, He will never let us go. When He seeks to have His way with us, surrender is the best and only way!

I loved my friends, my work, my home, my southern California lifestyle, and my financial income. It allowed me to travel to see my children and grandchildren whenever I wished. I began journaling every day, praying and listening. I keenly watched for those He sent on my path. My two entrepreneurial sons-in-law offered great suggestions for ministry work in the north and south of the country. My daughters each desired my presence in the lives of my grandchildren, all of which I took to prayer. If the truth be known, I would often argue with myself, finding part of me wasn't willing to give up my lifestyle and everything that went along with it.

Newport Coast teammates

Commit thy way unto the Lord,
  Trust also in Him, and He will do it.

         — Psalm 37:5

I knew God would be faithful to meet me when I was obedient and steadfast to know His will, yet I struggled with a sense of feeling as if I were stuck in the mud. I was full of anxiety, doubt, and fear about where He would call me, yet I knew the Lord was changing my desires to align with His.

It was during this time that I experienced two vivid nightmares, back-to-back. One was of me driving my late husband's car along a cliff. As I got too close to the edge, I went flying into an abyss, seeing my entire world beneath me in slow motion. I cried out to the Lord that I didn't want to die, but to live for Him. I floated over my world for what seemed forever. I never hit the ground; I just kept slowly floating sideways. I presumed I had died in the dream. I woke up in shock, as though thrown back into my bed. I lay there for a long time with my heart pounding!

The second nightmare came the next night. I dreamt I was like a bear being chased, running for its life. I frantically clung to the trunk of a high tree for fear of falling into the raging waters below and being swept downstream with the water washing over me, forcing me beneath the surface. I woke up from this dream in a cold sweat, once again with heart pounding!

I happened to be seeing my capable Christian counselor the next morning. He said, "Jo, this is 'Big Dream' material! Not only are they meaningful dreams, but you're dreaming in such a big way that it would spiritually amaze you!" He went on to explain that in dreams, death means rebirth and new life. When my car went over the precipice in the first dream, I surrendered to Christ and began a new life.

*Now faith is being sure of what we hope for,
being convinced of what we do not see.*

— Hebrews 11:1

In the later dream, he explained it was not the "tree of fear" I was clinging to, but rather the "tree of Marriott." He explained I wouldn't be giving up a career and income, I would be gaining time and a life to do His will, exactly what I had been praying for these past many months.

I had decisions to make. I called my boss and asked for the next two days off, (which he granted, since I had never made such a request). I went home, packed a light bag, and drove out to Palm Desert. I needed to get away to think, pray, and rest. I was exhausted with myself in every way.

HIS REDEMPTION : SURRENDER ON THE 55 FREEWAY

I arrived in Palm Desert in the cool of the evening and checked into a Marriott hotel, thankful my cozy room opened onto a quiet golf course and large pond. It was a lovely evening with a full moon. The stars filled the night sky, reflecting on the water as frogs croaked around the lily pads. I absentmindedly observed a couple walking hand in hand along the water's edge. I remember the prayer I offered with a dose of self-pity: "Oh, dear Lord, am I to be alone forever with no one to talk to and walk with on a lovely evening?"

My heart ached as I caught myself, tears stinging my eyes. I thanked God for being able to cry over my loss of Don, being assured by the Holy Spirit that my heart was still alive and overflowing with love for my children and grandchildren. I awoke with the dawn, walked up to the hotel to get a café latte, when my cell phone rang. It was my Coeur d'Alene son-in-law, Brandon, saying he had a big surprise for me.

"Meghan and I and the kids are all flying into Orange County today to be with you for a few weeks. We know you're wrestling with things right now. We just want to be there to support you, fill your house with the kids, and give you lots of hugs! We'll arrive in time for dinner."

Oh, my, I thought! My house is empty, my dog is in the kennel, there's no food or sweets in the refrigerator for my grandbabies, and no flowers to freshen and welcome their arrival!

I threw my things together, checked out of the hotel and got on the road. As I drove on the 55 Freeway, I thought, what am I teaching my children and grandchildren? That life is all about working six or seven days a week? That it's about making great money to put into retirement while not having time to pour into those you love the most? I had no time and no life!

For three years, I had come home every night to an empty house, except for my precious golden retriever, Amazing Grace. All I did was work, work, work. Weekend work was required, so I had not been to church in many months. My fellowship embers were dying.

I felt the conviction of the Holy Spirit as I drove. A kaleidoscope of my "life pictures" swirled before my eyes. I found myself crying, driving, and talking to my Lord of my precious Savior, my Hound of Heaven, and my Faithful God who had come to save me! After driving for an hour and a half, as I neared home, I was sobbing uncontrollably, and I didn't care who saw me! I lifted my heart up to the Lord and pleaded with Him to forgive me for having wandered so far off track.

WHAT CAN I GIVE YOU, LORD?

I surrender it all to you, Lord! Like what, Jo? I started letting go of it all:
"You can have my Marriott career, my income, my security for the future!"
"You can have my house—and You know how much I love my house!"
"You can have my California lifestyle...shopping, theatre, eating out(!),
   spending time with friends.
"You can even have California, Lord." Oh, goodness! What am I saying?

Then Jacob departed from Beersheba and went toward Haran. And he came to a certain place and spent the night there, because the sun had set; and he took one of the stones of the place and put it under his head, and lay down in that place. And he had a dream, and behold, a ladder was set on the earth with its top reaching to heaven; and behold, the angels of God were ascending and descending on it. And behold, the Lord stood above it and said, "I AM the Lord, the God of your father Abraham and the God of Isaac; the land on which you lie, I will give it to you and to your descendants. Your descendants shall also be like the dust of the earth and you shall spread out to the west and to the east and to the north and to the south; and in your descendants shall all the families of the earth be blessed. And behold I AM with you, and will keep you wherever you go, and will bring you back to this land; for I will not leave you until I have done what I have promised you." Then Jacob awoke from his sleep and said, "Surely the Lord is in this place and I did not know it." And he was afraid and said, "How awesome is this place! This is none other than the house of God and this is the gate of heaven."

So Jacob rose early in the morning and took the stone that he had put under his head and set it up as a pillar, and poured oil on its top. And he called the name of that place Bethel; however, previously the name of the city had been Luz. Then Jacob made a vow, saying, "If God will be with me and keep me on this journey that I take and will give me food to eat and garments to wear, and I return to my father's house in safety, then the Lord will be my God. And this stone, which I have set up as a pillar, will be God's house; and of all that Thou dost give me I will surely give a tenth to Thee.

— *Genesis 28:10-22*

"You can have my Lexus, too," the one I drove over the cliff in my nightmare.

I couldn't think of anything else I could give Him that I felt I was holding onto. Exhausted, I was quiet for a while. Then I felt the metaphorical tap on my shoulder.

"That's not all, Jo…"

I thought for a moment.

"Oh, no! You want my new Jaguar car, too? Ok, take it! Take it all! You can have it all!" I had saved seven years for that car and paid cash for it. *"All I want is to be in your will, Lord!"*

As I drove in silence, it dawned on me that I had earned all that income when we most needed it. But we were in such need that I had not paid my tithes to the Lord. I truly gasped as I promised to pay seven years of past tithes!

I was totally spent. But as I drove the last several miles home in silence, a warmth and peace came over me and within me unlike anything I had ever experienced in my entire life. Everything became crystal clear in my mind. I knew God had heard my prayer.

There comes a crisis-hour to each of us, if God has called us to the highest and the best, when all resources fail; when we face either ruin or something higher than we have ever dreamed; when we must have infinite help from God, and yet, ere we can have it, we must let something go; we must surrender completely; we must cease from our own wisdom, strength, and righteousness, and become crucified with Christ and alive in Him. God knows how to lead us up to this crisis, and He knows how to lead us through. Cast yourself helplessly at His feet.

Die to your strength and wisdom in His loving arms and rise, like Jacob, into His strength and all-sufficiency. There is no way out of your hard and narrow place but at the top. You must get deliverance by rising higher and coming into a new experience with God.

— Streams in the Desert, August 20

I knew God had taken me on my desert journey these past several years to humble me and test me, to take my roots deep in the search for living water. I thanked God for not asking me to sell everything and go to some forlorn country. He did, however, ask me to get rid of everything that had become more important to me than Him and His will for my life.

GOOD-BYE, SECURITY!

Brandon, Meghan, and my grandbabies—four of them under five years old—arrived that afternoon. The house was alive again with squeals and laughter, running in and out of rooms, up and down the stairs, indoors and out. They were so happy to be out of the Idaho winter and into the California sun! Once we had the kids in bed for the evening, Brandon, Meghan, and I sat outdoors by my fire pit. The phone rang. It was my Atlanta son-in-law, Steve!

"Guess what? I'm going to be in Orange County for business tomorrow. How 'bout letting me take you out for dinner?"

"I'd love it!" I answered, with a big smile on my face. Thank You, Lord! God always seems to send us just who we need, just when we need them.

After two incredible evenings discussing the timeframe of my career exit with my daughter and two sons-in-law, I reached a decision. The next morning, I walked into my boss's office with my written resignation in hand. Unaware of my encounter with God on the 55 Freeway, he would not accept my resignation! He knew the stress and strain that accompanied our work. He told me to take the next two weeks off. "I'm sure you'll be ready to come back to work then, Jo."

I remember the calm and peace with which I said, "Thanks, I'll do that, but I know this is what the Lord wants for me. I'll be in touch, but I won't be coming back. God's called me, although I know not where. I want to be free to heed His call."

I was blessed to have a great boss, who had taught me everything I knew in our business. He understood who I was and how determined (stubborn) I could be at times! He gave me his blessing and asked me to call him every Friday.

HIS REFINING : THE SUMMER OF MY COCOON

The summer of 2005 brought a season of expectant waiting. Waiting on the Lord is often necessary to see Him clearly. We need to sit at His feet regularly. Our lives must occasionally be restful and quiet. I loved the sunsets during the "summer of my cocoon." I had decided to withdraw into the stillness of His world. I wanted to be quiet, to silence the noise and distractions of a busy work life so I could hear His whisper in my heart. I devoted myself to prayer, fasting, and God's Word.

I will give myself unto prayer.

— *Psalm 109:4*

The peace of God must quiet our minds and rest our hearts. We must place our hand in the hand of God like a little child, and let Him lead us out into the bright sunshine of His love and will for our lives.

— *Streams in the Desert, October 7*

There is something
wonderfully sacred
that happens when
a woman chooses to look
past being set aside
to see God's call for her
to be set apart.

— Lysa TerKeurst

"We need to learn also to wait on God for the unfolding of His will. Let God form your plans about everything in your mind and heart and then let Him execute them. Sometimes it may seem so contradictory to the plan He gave. Simply listen, obey and trust God, even when things seem folly to do so. He will make "all things work together for His good."

— Streams in the Desert, October 3

Dear Reader, perhaps your circumstances have led you to seek a solitary place. Take that solitude as God's gift to you and learn to know Him during the time you set aside for study and meditation. Paul spent three years in Arabia after his transformation learning more about God before God called him to his kingdom work. I knew that to find my calling, I had to let go of everything to be still and hear His voice.

And do not be conformed to this world,
but be transformed by the renewing of your mind,
that you may prove what the will of God is,
that which is good and acceptable and perfect.

— Romans 12:2

Oh, how difficult it is to wait upon God! I remember the pain and grief of placing myself in God's will as an act of obedience and trust. I knew only God could bring beauty and life out of the ashes and the loneliness of missing my daughters, sons-in-law, and my precious grandchildren! How God has blessed us all! The Holy Spirit guided me and gave me time to learn of Him, and kept me from stumbling. God can take a little and make much of it. I trusted that He would use my circumstances to teach me, train me, and prepare me for His calling.

My friend, don't ever underestimate what God can do in your life when you surrender and yield yourself completely to Him. He has the best plan possible for your life. When things seem impossible, instead of wringing your hands like I did when Steve and Shannon moved to Baltimore, when Brandon and Meghan moved to Coeur d'Alene, when Don had tongue cancer, when Don passed on, seek God's will. Ask Him, "What are You going to do, Lord?"

BEGGING GOD TO REVEAL MY CALLING

I was already a believer and follower of our Lord, Jesus Christ. I reset my compass to devote myself to living a holy life for Him. I vowed to be faithful and responsible to Him, to be fruitful and seek God's will for my life, and to hear His call for me to do what no one else but I could do. I knew He had made me for His purpose.

I felt both set apart and set aside. I experienced days of loneliness and fear of the future, sometimes doubting whether or not God would keep His promise to me. But I knew God was who He said He was and that He would do what He said He would do.

Steve and Shannon had asked me to pray about moving to Atlanta to be close to them and my grandchildren. I could move to Coeur d'Alene, or I could move to Atlanta, but how in the world would I ever explain to my grandchildren why I chose one over the other? I had nightmares about it! I promised my daughters I would seek the Lord's will on where I would move. I brought my empty vessel before Him in faith and prayer, praise, and adoration. I was quiet and patient, taking one day at a time. My life was on hold.

I came to remember that the Spirit has not only a service of work, but a service of waiting. Sometimes we may be called to do nothing, to work by keeping still, to serve by waiting.

When I cannot understand my Father's leading

And it seems to be but a hard and cruel fate,

Still I hear that gentle whisper ever pleading,

God is working, God is faithful, only wait."

— *George Matheson*

When God speaks to you, revealing what He is about to do, that revelation is your invitation to adjust your life to Him. Once you have adjusted your life to Him, His purposes, and His ways, you are in a position to obey. Adjustments prepare you for obedience. You cannot continue life as usual or stay where you are, and go with God at the same time. It is true throughout Scripture. Some even had to leave family and home or country.

— *Henry Blackaby & Claude V. King, Experiencing God (pg. 234)*

BIBLE MARGIN: August, 2005

"Through this summer of cocooning, God has revealed His desire for my obedience and humility…to strive to be holy as He is holy, to tell our family that God is faithful and will not destroy His covenant with us…to live according to the Law of God, to be obedient to His Laws."

HIS PREPARATION : I HAVE A NEW LIFE FOR YOU

One morning in my quiet time, I wrote down all of the volunteer and work-related activities I had participated in the past, attempting to find a consistent theme or purpose. Most of my life had been filled with teaching and training. My college education prepared me for a teaching career. I taught elementary school children for four years, going right into the seasons of marriage and motherhood, while also teaching and training expectant mothers in my La Maze Prepared Childbirth classes at the hospital. My business provided occasions for teaching and training my staff and clients at William Ernest Brown and Jo King & Co. in the ways of social invitations, writing, and gift giving. When cancer entered our lives, my daughter, Meghan, and I managed Don's medical office. When we were bankrupt, God had given me Coldwell Banker Real Estate with a high learning curve and training that prepared me to become Training Team Leader at Marriott Coast Villas.

What stood out was a common thread throughout my work and volunteer experiences—relationships. I realized that relationships with people were my passion. I discovered—on that memorable first Saturday off in seven years—God had prepared me to do His work after all! He had given me a heart and a passion for people, my family, and the desire to bless and help others heal through His Holy Spirit.

For we are God's workmanship,
created in Christ Jesus to do good works,
which God has prepared in advance for us to do.

— Ephesians 2:10

As timing would have it, I was also working on my Master's Program notebook on Kingdom Calling. As I wrote in my notebook that morning:

MASTER'S NOTEBOOK: 2004

"Lord, my heart is for women and children, to bless and to heal. I would love to be a speaker and writer for You...to tell others of Your mercy, grace, love and faithfulness to all! I want to give them hope, Who is Christ Jesus."

THE GOD OF SURPRISES

I knew, without a doubt, that His promises were true and that He would reveal His purpose and plan for my life in His time.

Do not call to mind the former things,
Or ponder things of the past.
BEHOLD, I WILL DO SOMETHING NEW,
Now it will spring forth;
Will you not be aware of it?
I will even make a roadway in the wilderness,
Rivers in the desert.

— Isaiah 43:18-19

I heard His call:

"Come with Me, Jo. Give up everything and come with Me.
Your Kingdom work awaits you!"

I began to move!

It has not yet appeared what we shall be.

— *1 John 3:2*

delight,

ANGELS WELCOME HERE

GRACE NOTES | *Surrender and Renewal*

- Remember: first comes surrender, then comes renewal.

- The pain of grief is a great teacher. We can surrender our pain to the Lord, but then we need to get up and move in our pain. Our help comes from the Lord. Ask Him to see you through.

- When God is preparing us for a new thing, His loving hands prune us to produce greater fruit, to be stronger and better than we are today. Let Him have His way with you.

- We all have our day of Total Surrender on the calendar. When you are at the end of yourself, the Lord will be there to fill your empty vessels and reset the direction of your life with His desire and His Purpose.

- There are major, life-changing moments of surrender in our lives; but there also is the practice of moment-by-moment, day-by-day surrender on the journey. Both are invaluable.

- When we are no longer able to control our circumstances, we are challenged to change ourselves. It's a call from complacency...time to grow your faith again.

- The "summer of your cocoon" (or however the Lord guides you) trains you in humility, obedience, and discipline. Though uncomfortable at times, it can give you clarity about His Purpose for your life after grief. God is a loving Father and He knows our need before we tell Him. Surrender your needs to Him.

- Broken, empty vessels are best suited for receiving new blessings. It is the Law of Divine Supply.

- To God, the darkest depths of the human heart are as clear as the page of a book lying open in the sunlight. God sees us and knows us. Trust Him to renew your spirit. The lessons of deep and unbearable grief will be used for His Kingdom calling.

- Our loved ones will always be close in our hearts. One day you will awake and find you have been prepared to move, in spite of your pain, to turn the lessons of grief into your harvest season for blessing others. You will be surrendered, renewed, and equipped. Go out to do what God made you to do and do it for His glory!

*Weeping may endure for a night,
but joy cometh in the morning.*

— **Psalm 30:5**

STONE 10   BLESSING AND FAVOR

*T*he story of Don Jackson began long before I arrived on the scene. God had been preparing him as well as me. I thought, Dear Reader, that hearing a little of his journey to our love story might enrich your understanding of God's faithfulness and appreciation for His abundant blessings.

Don is a farmer, a man who loves to work with the land. Throughout the 1960s, 70s, and 80s, he bought and developed farmland. He sold a few ranches and did well financially, which enabled him and his wife Pat to travel extensively. Their passions for God's work sent them all over the world with Campus Crusade for Christ—the Philippines, Malaysia, Singapore, Kuala Lampur. They also took their two sons, Steve and Robert, and their daughter, Julie, to Africa and Europe, almost always with a mission to share the gospel.

By the early 80s, Don was farming over 28,000 acres and involved in all sorts of business projects. He always had a visionary gift for business and poured himself into his work and his family. At the home ranch on the Kings River in Kingsburg, he and Pat would routinely host gatherings of hundreds of people in the "back yard by the river," so life was always full of guests and family activities. After Steve and Robert were married, and with Julie away in college, Don and Pat had a few years of time with just each other, traveling, serving, and enjoying God's blessings. But while returning from a trip in October of 1993, Pat began feeling extremely tired—not just worn out, but completely drained. When rest didn't solve the problem, the neurologist insisted she see a specialist at the University of San Francisco Medical Hospital to further diagnose the problem. The next day they sat in his office. Within five minutes he delivered the diagnosis—ALS or Lou Gehrig's disease. Stunned, Don asked the doctor what could be done to treat it. "I'm sorry," he replied. "Absolutely nothing. She has a year or two."

As Don came to discover, ALS (Amyotrophic Lateral Sclerosis), also known as Lou Gehrig's disease (named after the famous baseball player who had it), is a progressive autoimmune disease that basically attacks your body's ability to function. It is a neurodegenerative disease that affects nerve cells in the brain and spinal cord. It often begins to show itself in one's arms or legs and over time affects vital organs. When it moves to the lungs, there is nothing anyone can do. By February, the doctor had come to meet with the family to explain that no one had ever survived the disease and eventually, if Pat were to live, she would need to be on a respirator all the time.

They had heard of a doctor in Australia who might be of help. She had been the personal physician for Tito, the Yugoslavian dictator, before she had escaped to the West. She had followed her daughter to Australia and set up practice, so Don and Pat traveled "down under" to be under her care. Once Pat tried to share her faith in God, the doctor gruffly replied, "I'm an atheist, don't talk to me about it." But Pat cared so deeply for people, she was never one to take no for an answer when it really mattered.

Don and Pat got to know her and her husband well over the next three months, building a relationship with them. When it was time to head back to the US, the doctor told Pat to come back if she got well. If not, she said she would come to Pat.

Don struggled greatly to make sense of it all. Pat was the person who really seemed to make a difference with people while Don was a go-getter. Why, he thought, would God take Pat and not him? He wrestled with anger even as he brought her

ALWAYS IN OUR HEARTS

home, with him and Julie caring for her and making the most of the time they had. He and Julie struggled as the end drew near.

When Pat didn't get better, true to her word, the doctor and her husband came to Kingsburg. They stayed with Don's brother, George, and his wife, Colleen, for ten days, helping to care for Pat. When Pat passed in July of 1994, at the young age of fifty-three, the doctor was in the bed next to her. Even in death, Pat had deeply touched another life with God's love.

Coping with Pat's loss was especially difficult for Don and Julie. Julie and her mom had been extremely close, and she found herself without her mother at the early age of twenty-three.

Don had grown up in a home where his mother was always present. He had been married to Pat since he was only twenty, so he had always known her to be there in the home throughout their thirty-four years of marriage. She kept the house feeling like a home and was always at the center of everything from events to relationships. So her passing left a tremendous void in Don's life. He had an immensely supportive family—his children, his siblings, and his parents all loved on him—but he never really got intentional about dealing with his grief. He poured himself into his work and continued to travel a great deal. His work and friends with Campus Crusade helped pull him through a season of anger and depression.

Over the next twelve years, Don made the journey through unexpected and difficult widowhood. It wasn't easy. In the ensuing grief of losing a beloved spouse, there is tremendous loneliness and isolation paired with the impossible adjustment of coming home to an empty house. We are left with an intense longing to still be loved and connected and are often suseptible to making relationship mistakes. But through God's grace, we are forgiven.

Don and his best friend John

After thou hast patiently endured,

    thou shall receive the promise.

The moment of supreme sacrifice

    shall be the moment of supreme blessing.

God's river, which is FULL OF WATER,

    shall burst it's banks

and pour upon thee a tide of wealth and grace.

    There is nothing, indeed,

which God will not do for a man

    who dares to step out upon

what seems to be the midst;

    though as he puts down his foot

he finds a STONE beneath him.

    — F.B. Meyer

HIS PROVIDENCE : THERE ONCE WAS A MAN FROM KINGSBURG

My daughter, Shannon, and son-in-law, Steve, were due any moment. They were going on a two-week trip to Southeast Asia with The Founders Group of the Ravi Zacharias Ministry and blessing me with the care of my four precious grandchildren. I had taken a hiatus from my cocoon to enjoy this priceless gift. I put off all decisions of where to move until after we had filled the two weeks with fun days and movie nights and as much of Grandma's homemade buttered popcorn as we could stand.

On a beautiful July morning, I left all my cares and concerns at the foot of Jesus.

Delight yourself in the Lord,
And He will give you the desires of your heart.

— Psalm 37:4

I thought I would be helpful. "Well, Lord, just in case You have a plan for me to marry again, I'll make a list of what's important to me, so I'll recognize him when he comes!" I set about writing a list:

I'd love someone who ...
- *Loves You, Lord, first and foremost*
- *Loves their family as I love mine*
- *Already knows how to make a good marriage, preferably a widower*
- *Has a big, loving heart and is gentle, humble, and kind*
- *Has an abundant spirit*
- *Has an abundance of energy and a sense of adventure, so we could see our grandchildren whenever we wish*
- *Has an abundance of friends and family*

- *Has an abundance of love for You, Lord, with a desire to give to the Kingdom*
- *Has an abundance of love for me, Lord, that he will delight in and cherish me, grateful You brought us into each other's life*
- *Is smart and well-read with a great sense of humor to take us through the rest of our journey*
- *(As an extra treat) would love beautiful music and Broadway theatre...and opera!*

I slipped the list into the middle of my Bible and eagerly started preparing for my family's arrival. With my little Grandes in tow (ages 12, 9, 6, and 4), we went to the park, the beach, Balboa Island, Fashion Island, and visited friends and family. Every evening, Steve and Shannon called from Southeast Asia, checking in on how the kids were doing. Each excitedly took turns talking to Daddy and Mama. It was the best of times, and the days passed all too quickly.

The night before Steve and Shannon were leaving for the long flight home, Shannon called: "Mom, Steve and I have been looking far and wide for the perfect gift to bring home to you. We finally found it!"

"Honey, I don't want you to bring anything home to me! Having my grandchildren for the past two weeks has been the greatest gift of all."

"I know the kids have enjoyed it, Mom, but Steve and I are so excited. This Gift is Priceless! We're bringing home your new husband!" I still get goose bumps when I think of it, just as I did when Shannon said those words.

"Mom, George and Colleen have a widowed brother, and Colleen and I have been doing our due diligence and deep discovery on you both. We think you sound perfectly suited for one another! And get this, Mom! His name is Don—

Don Jackson. He lives on the Kings River in Kingsburg, where you spent those six months a few years ago. You loved it!"

Of course, my late husband's name was Don King. After he had retired from his full-time medical practice, he did a locum tenens assignment for a physician with an office up in the Central Valley of California farm country near Kingsburg. I had loved our time there, away from the hubbub of city life.

"I'll tell you all about him when we get home tomorrow night, Mom, but he sounds wonderfully suited for you, loves adventure, loves to travel—and he's George's brother, so we know he's a great guy!"

Steve and Shannon had been acquainted with the Jacksons for three or four years and loved being with them. Steve had even been up to the Jackson home in Kingsburg and had come back to our house laden with boxes of fruit!

"The four of us think it would be great for you both to meet in November at The Founders Weekend in Washington D.C. The six of us can have dinner and get acquainted!"

Well, I trusted my daughter. She definitely sounded confident. I had not dated anyone for some time. When friends tried to set me up with anyone, I honestly answered, "If God wants me to marry again, he'll just show up at my door." I was quite content with praying about whether or not the Lord wanted me to move!

Certainty is the mark of the common-sense life; gracious uncertainty is the mark of the spiritual life. To be certain of God means that we are uncertain in all our ways, we do not know what a day may bring forth. This is generally said with a sigh of sadness; it should be rather an expression of breathless expectation. We are uncertain of the next step, but we are certain of God.

So, as those who have been chosen of God,
    holy and beloved, put on a heart of compassion,
kindness, humility, gentleness and patience;
    bearing with one another, and forgiving each other,
whoever has a complaint against anyone;
    just as the Lord forgave you, so also should you.
Beyond all these things put on love,
    which i the perfect bond of unity.
Let the peace of Christ rule in your hearts,
    to which indeed you were called in one body;
and be thankful.

— *Colossians 3:12-15*

Immediately we abandon to God, and do the duty that lies nearest, He packs our life with surprises all the time.

— My Utmost for His Highest, April 29

GOD'S MIRACLES COME IN SILENCE, UNANNOUNCED

The first call from Mr. Don Jackson came just four days later on a quiet Sunday evening. He introduced himself and asked if he had called at a good time. That impressed me, right there! He went on to say he had been out for dinner with his brother and sister-in-law the night before. They had told him about the matchmaking going on in Southeast Asia the past two weeks. They had also shown him a picture of me sent by fax from my son-in-law. "I've seen your beautiful picture and it made my heart skip! I'm very excited to meet you."

"Oh, my! Just what photograph did my son-in-law send to you?"

"Well, I think it's one of you and your daughter sitting in a field. You're wearing a cowboy hat."

"That must be when we were at the Dude Ranch last summer. Oh, dear, I didn't know he sent you a picture!"

After we chatted a while longer, he said, "Well, since neither of us have any time to waste, I'd like to ask you a few questions, if you don't mind. Things that are really important to me." I agreed. "I understand from your daughter and son-in-law you are a Godly woman and you love the Lord. Is that true?"

"Yes, I love the Lord with all my heart."

"And I understand you're a strong family woman, too, who loves to spend time with her children and grandchildren."

"Yes, my children and grandchildren are more important to me than anyone or anything in this earthly life."

"Well, I agree, and I'm happy to hear that."

"Now, the next question could be a deal breaker because it's a big part of who I am. I'd like to know whether you're a Liberal or a Conservative!"

"Oh, goodness, you've got to be kidding! I live in Orange County—the Conservative Bubble of Southern California!"

"Thank goodness, because I took a gal out for dinner a few months ago and, just two blocks from her house, she told me how much she liked Michael Moore!"

"What did you do?" I asked.

"Why, I turned the car right around and said, 'Lady, you and I have nothing in common, so there's no sense in wasting each other's time!"

"You mean, you didn't even take her out for dinner?"

"No, that dinner would not have been good!"

Good thing I'm not a fan of Michael Moore, I thought.

We talked awhile longer, enjoying the conversation as I asked the same first two questions of him. Don was a widower, so we each shared about our experience in losing a spouse. Finally, he said he enjoyed our conversation and would call the next day.

Don called early in the morning—and early in the evening—for three more days. We had long, heartfelt conversations about our families, children, and work. The morning of the third day, he said, "You know, I think we should get together sooner rather than waiting until November! We could be wasting a lot of time between now and then. Besides, we need to find out whether these matchmakers have done a good job or not! I'd like to drive down tomorrow afternoon, if you're available. If you can find me a hotel, I'll make reservations for dinner tomorrow evening. If we enjoy one another, I'll stay for the weekend, so we can get to know each other better. If not, you can send me home with my tail between my legs!"

I was quite eager to meet this guy! I liked his strength of character and honesty. He had an easy-going, humble way about him, too.

"It might be difficult to get a hotel room in Newport Beach in August," I replied. "The city swells to about 70,000 in the summer."

"Well, since I don't know the area, will you please call around for me and give me about four choices?"

I called my daughter, Shannon, as soon as I got off the phone to tell her the good news, knowing my other daughter was busy with four babies under five years old. "Well, Mom," Shannon advised, "you need to find him four, very nice hotels so he knows your style!"

I called him back with the four hotel choices, and, wouldn't you know it, he picked the most expensive one! "I've always heard about that beautiful hotel. I think that would be perfect for our first date." Swoon!

JOURNAL: August 18, 2005

Today I meet Mr. Don Jackson! He's a widower and "quite a catch" from what they say. He's driving down from Kingsburg, (Don from Kingsburg) to spend a few days to meet one another. He's a gentleman, loves the Lord, and has a great sense of humor, three children, and eleven grandchildren. He's adventuresome and loves to travel. I'm anxious to meet him, Lord!"

HIS TIMING : FOUR DAYS THAT CHANGED OUR WORLD

I volunteered at Hoag Hospital on Thursday, but asked to take off early to go home and shower, do my hair, and prepare for our date. Our volunteer uniforms consisted of white pants, a navy "Volunteer" jacket and white tennis shoes—not exactly a first date "dress-to-impress" outfit. So you can imagine my shock when I walked through my back garage door and into my kitchen—only to see Don Jackson ringing the doorbell at my front door!

I had no place to hide! I opened the door, smiling, as I said, "Are you Don? You're an hour early. I'm just getting home from the hospital!" He was standing tall and strong at my door, holding a close-to-dead plant from my front porch in his hand.

He just smiled and said, "Well, you just take your time getting ready. I'll go into the kitchen and water your poor plant."

I told him to make himself at home in the living room. As I walked upstairs, I said to myself, *He thinks he's here to water my plant, but I know the Lord has sent him to water my soul.* I just knew. And I remembered my earlier comment: *He'll just show up at my door....*

We talked easily as we drove south to Laguna Beach. Driving onto the beautiful Montage Hotel property along the majestic clear blue ocean coastline was breathtaking. Don asked me what my girls thought of us going on our first date. I laughed and told him we had been talking just about every hour! Since our dinner reservations weren't until seven o'clock, we sat out on the patio of his room, in awe of the beautiful ocean view.

My phone rang. Apparently, my girls couldn't wait another moment to get the verdict. They had advised me earlier of their special code: if I thought he was great, I was to say I was wearing a green dress; if I wasn't interested, I was to say I was wearing a red dress. As he sat beside me, I had a light conversation with them before they asked me "the dress question." "Green!" They cheered so loud I was sure Don could hear them.

When I finished our phone call, he got a big grin on his face: "Looks like I passed the first checkpoint with you and your daughters!"

As we were seated at a small table for two outside of The Studio restaurant on the

MONTAGE MEMORIES

water, Don took a deep breath, inhaling the clear, clean ocean air. "This is so beautiful and peaceful, and we're just in time to see the sunset."

When our food arrived, Don reached for my hand, saying, "Shall we pray?" I was struck by his strong, large hands, warm smile, and beautiful Irish eyes. Then I was touched by his prayer, whispered into the fresh ocean air, blessing our food and our time together and asking that our conversation would honor God. From the very first hour together, it was extraordinary and delightful!

Three and a half hours later, we realized we were the only ones left in the restaurant. We had decided against dessert, but Don had ordered French press coffee— my favorite! Lisa, our attentive and amazing waitress, suddenly placed a large and beautiful chocolate swan dessert before us!

"Oh, you decided to order dessert?" I asked.

"No," said Don. "Did you?"

Lighting the candle on the swan, Lisa gave us a knowing big, beautiful smile. "Happy Anniversary, you two lovebirds!" Don and I looked at each other and started laughing.

"Lisa, do you know how long I've known this beautiful lady?"

"Well," said Lisa, "we've all been in the kitchen watching you all evening, so touched by your love for each other…we're guessing twenty to twenty-five years?"

"How about three hours!" Don told the story of our meeting and our family who had done the matchmaking from Southeast Asia. "And here we are!"

Lisa still had the shocked look on her face. "Wait 'til I tell everyone. We've all been amazed by your love for one another."

"I'll tell you what, Lisa," Don said "If we ever do celebrate an anniversary, we'll be sure to return and collect our candle from you!"

As we enjoyed our chocolate swan and French pressed coffee, Don slipped the napkin from beneath his cup, took out his pen and said, "I wasn't going to ask you this until the end of the weekend, but what would a beautiful lady like you look for in a marriage relationship?"

"As a matter of fact," I replied, "I recently wrote some things down not too long ago." He wrote as I listed what was on the note tucked away in my Bible at home. After a moment, I slipped the napkin from beneath my cup and asked him the same question.

Don and I have celebrated almost twelve anniversaries since that night and five of them have been sitting at Lisa's table at The Studio of the Montage Hotel in Laguna Beach, California. And we each kept those napkins in our wallets until they disintegrated!

HIS SAFETY : THINGS ONLY GOD KNOWS

I need to share this aside with you, Dear Reader, and with my grandchildren, because God knows certain things about each of us that only He knows. I had a fear. It was an unfounded fear, but real to me, nonetheless. Being alone and widowed, I worried if I ever dated anyone, and they brought me home at the end of the evening, they would slip in my door without an invitation, and I would not be able to get them to leave! I had never had a stranger in my house after dark. As I said, my fear was unfounded, but real to me.

Consequently, when Don walked me up to my front door at the end of our evening, I could feel my anxiety rising. Touching me gently on the shoulder, Don thanked me for a most wonderful evening.

"Do you have your key?" he asked, holding out his hand.

"Oh! Yes," I said, as I handed him the key. He unlocked my Dutch door, gently pushing it open ahead of me.

"I'll look forward to seeing you in the morning. I'll be at the Pageant of the Masters ticket window before they open to get us tickets, so you won't have to drive down to Laguna. Sleep well!" He smiled, handing me the key as he closed the door behind me.

As I finally exhaled, I stood there amazed. What a gentleman! More than that, the Lord knew how much it meant to me to be able to trust this man.

JOURNAL: August 18, 2005

My first evening with Don tonight, from the first hour, was easy, comfortable, warm and SAFE. He's strong, gentle, sincere, humble, loving, wonderful with other people, conversational, and has beautiful eyes and an easy-going gait—almost like a cowboy! He's tall, handsome, kind, ATTENTIVE, and SAFE! Thank You, Lord!

LET DOWN YOUR WINGS

When Shannon called early the next morning, I relayed the details of our evening together. I told her I'd keep her and Meghan up-to-date. I mentioned a reading from Ezekiel 1:25 in my Streams in the Desert devotional several weeks earlier on June 17th, that kept running through my mind throughout that evening. The passage described a moment heard in heaven.

And when they went, I heard the noise of their wings,
like the noise of great waters, as the voice of the Almighty,
the voice of speech, as the noise of an host:
when they stood still, they lowered their wings.

— Ezekiel 1:24

"Honey, I felt that for the first time in ten years, I could truly let down my wings. I felt the calm, rest, and peace of the Lord's hand upon me, beckoning me to 'Be still and trust.'"

Following a lovely Saturday breakfast at the hotel the next morning, Don and I took a long walk on the beach. Sitting on a large boulder, we began sharing about our lives and our children. I had been sharing about the girls, their swim team, and sabot sailing lessons at the Yacht Club, when Don said, "Tell me about your favorite season of your life, Jo."

"That's easy," I told him. "My favorite years were raising our girls with all the memories with family and friends. All our lives revolved around water. Whether growing up on a lake in Wisconsin, spending vacations on a lake with my family, fishing with my dad in California, or all the years of our summers, sailing from Alamitos Bay to Catalina, racing with friends and their families to be the first ones there, trips to Hawaii, and all our family times together—those were my favorite memories and seasons of life. I would never want to live away from the water. It's like my life-blood to be around an ocean or lake."

Silence. I almost thought Don had not been listening as he looked out at the ocean. Finally, he turned his gaze from the water to me, looked down into my face, and softly asked, "Will a river do?"

The weekend flew by in a carousel of coastline adventures—dining, strolling, and sightseeing. On Sunday morning, we made the drive to Rick Warren's Saddleback Church. We worshipped and praised our Lord together. Don took my hand frequently, as he had since our first date. I felt protected, loved, and cared for the first time in a long time. I wanted to cry for joy.

We checked Don out of the hotel and drove to my house to say good-bye before he returned home to Kingsburg. He hadn't been inside my house since the first day when he watered my plant. He asked to come in and go into the kitchen. "I need to share my thoughts with you." He hoisted himself up onto my kitchen island and asked me to come close.

Taking my hands tenderly into his, he said, "These past four days have been so incredible, Jo. I want you to know I care for you. I'm taken with your love for the Lord, your love of people, your spirit, and your joy. You are everything I've been looking for, for so many years. I truly believe the Lord brought us together. Now we need to pray, spend as much time as possible together to get to know each other. We need to ask questions of each other and follow His lead."

I agreed and said, "We can go as slowly as you wish."

He shared how he had made mistakes in the past and he and his entire family had suffered greatly for his foolishness and rebellion. "Jo, I want this to be right, for us, as well as for our families, so I'd like our relationship to be pure and celibate. I treasure you and I want more than anything to be right in God's eyes."

He bent down and kissed me for the first time! It was passionate, warm, and a kiss we will never forget.

"I guess you may have to slap my hand now and then!"

"Well then, I can tell you we won't be spending a lot of time at my house!" After thinking a moment, I added, "And we will do this for how long?"

"Until we can't stand it any longer...then we'll get married."

It was so difficult to say good-bye. We talked several times on his four-hour drive home. He asked to join me in Coeur d'Alene for Labor Day. I was leaving soon to see my daughter, son-in-law, and four grandchildren for two weeks. I told him I wanted to have the first ten days to be with them alone and fill my grandchildren's love tanks,

then he could fly up for the last four days.

"Well, I think it's definitely important for me to meet them, he said, "before we get more serious. I'd best find out if they approve of me, in case they ding me!"

FAMILY BLESSINGS

As I excitedly scanned the crowd at the airport, my eyes spotted Don coming down the ramp with a crate of fruit on each shoulder and a big grin on his face! We were so happy to finally see one another, even though we had spoken several times a day over the previous ten days. As he walked in their front door, he was met with smiles and hugs from everyone. The first thing Don did was get down on one knee to greet the three little girls running into his arms as though they had known him forever. Constant chatter filled the house as they helped him with the fruit and satchels, eagerly showing him to his room.

Once settled, we joined in the kitchen to sample the fruit he had laid out before us. Don spotted my granddaughter, Maddie, the oldest, looking over the options. "Maddie, I think you would really like this Asian pear. It's good and juicy!"

"No thank you, Mr. Jackson."

"Well, I just bet if you try it you would like it!"

Soon the juice dripped down her chin as she exclaimed, "This is the best fruit ever! Oh, Grammie, you just have to marry Mr. Jackson!"

Everyone burst into laughter! I was quite embarrassed for a nanosecond, then seeing the look on Don's face, I joined in the laughter!

We had a whirlwind-four-days all together, with trips around Hayden Lake in their boat with kids in life jackets, big smiles on all our faces, conversations

*Depart from your country and your relatives
and come to the land that I will show you.*

— Acts 7:2-4

PURE JOY

at dinner at Coeur d'Alene Resort, driving out to Green Bluff for some good ol' country music, Halloween Hay Mazes, and fresh peaches. Everyone loved him! Brandon, Meghan, and all my grandchildren gave us their blessing.

The next weekend, Don made the four-hour drive from Kingsburg to Newport again, this time to meet my sister and family—my only relatives living down south. My sister, Mary Jo and I are very close, so it meant a great deal to have her husband, Mike, and my nieces and nephews, all meet Don. We had a great night exchanging stories of his childhood and ours. They loved him and gave us their blessing.

Kingsburg was next! Don's children and their families had been traveling with summer vacations but would all be back home two weeks later. He assured me I would not have to meet them all at once. I would stay with his son, daughter-in-law, and their five children. That was plenty right there, but there were ten others with the other two children, plus all of Don's siblings and their families.

Before I left for such an undertaking, I sought the stable counsel of my friend and prayer partner, Natalie. We prayed together for some time, after which she said, "Jo, God has 'filled your life with all good instruction'. He has given you eyes to see and ears to hear. Now open your arms to heaven and say Yes! to all the blessings God is showering down on you!"

I left the next day with anticipation and excitement to meet Don's family. He had assured me his family knew about our relationship and looked forward to meeting me. He said he would meet me outside of Kingsburg so we could drive together as he "took me home." Little did I know, when I left Newport Beach that day, I was beginning the rest of my life in Kingsburg with Don Jackson!

The Lord said to Abram, 'Go…to the land I will show you.'

— *Genesis 12:1*

When once the call of

God comes, begin to go

and never stop going.

— *My Utmost*

for His Highest,

September 27

When God asked Abram to leave his homeland and family, He didn't offer much information concerning the destination. He gave no geographic coordinates, no description of the new land or the natural resources. Nor did he give an indication of how long it would take to get there. God simply gave the direction to go.

GOD HAD ME SURRENDER ALL, THEN HE MOVED ME

I knew I was adjusting my life to God and His plan for my life and my future. The Lord was the only one who could have had me leave my home and treasured life in Newport Beach for an unknown land. Often God brings us to the end of ourselves, develops our dependence on Him, so that our lives are surrendered to His will, not ours. I had sensed His leading to get ready to move. I thought it would be south to Atlanta, but it was north to the San Joaquin Valley! As Henry Blackaby put it, "You must make major adjustments in your life to join God in what He is doing."

On September 15, almost one month from our first date, I arrived in Kingsburg, ready to meet Don's family with only a "three-day-suitcase" and plans to stay with Don's son, Rob, and his wife, Sarah. We made our way to his daughter's house first where we were enthusiastically welcomed by Ryan, Julie, and their (then) two sons, just 3 and 5 years old! We laughed as we shared Jonas's nickname of JoJo and my nickname of Jo! The very next day, Friday, September 16, Don drove me to Shell Beach, where he had lived by the ocean while building his house in Kingsburg. Next to the bench on the beach where he used to read his daily newspaper, he got down on one knee and asked me to marry him! Of course, I said *yes*! (That's the short version!)

That evening, we drove back to Rob and Sarah's house. Being Rob's birthday, they had invited Rob's aunt, two uncles, and their spouses to celebrate his birthday

WEDDING PLANS

and "meet Dad's new love interest!" It was also the first time I actually met George and Colleen, the other half of the matchmakers. We laughed all evening long!

On Saturday, September 17, Don told me he would pick me up early for a surprise day. Leaving at seven in the morning, we drove up the coast in my new car (which I had previously surrendered to the Lord and planned to sell when I moved to Atlanta). Don drove with a smile on his face and intention in his spirit, yet he would not tell me what he had planned. As we drove down Ocean Avenue in the enchanting coastal village of Carmel, we parked in front of Fourtane Estate Jewelers. We walked past their old Rolex clock stand and large American Flag to enter the store. The antique wood floors creaked as we entered and were met by a lovely sales woman.

"We're here to look for wedding rings," Don revealed. I looked into the case and saw the perfect ring right away! When I showed it to Don, he agreed it was the perfect choice! He bought the ring, took me out to the car in the beautiful pouring rain, and placed the ring on my finger. Once again, he professed his love to me and I did the same to him. We then went to his favorite restaurant, Anton and Michel. Its fountain and fireplaces created the perfect setting for a romantic engagement dinner.

We drove home along Highway 1 through Big Sur, playing George Strait country songs and Andrea Bocelli Italian opera music. (Yes, God had even given me someone who loved opera!) We had talked earlier about my possibly renting an apartment in Visalia while we continued dating and getting to know one another. Now we looked at each other and laughed. We really didn't need any more time. We both knew that first date at the Montage that we wanted to spend the rest of our lives together!

Sunday, September 18, we attended Sunday Service at a small corner church in Kingsburg. We found ourselves surrounded by several "Jackson" families with small children, all introducing themselves as "family!" They were all so warm and welcoming. After a day of Don showing me around his treasured home of Kingsburg, we joined his family at Cafe 225, in Visalia, where his son and daughter in law, Steve and Sue, lived with their four children. We were all together. Don's two sons, one daughter, their wives and husband, and all of Don's grandchildren, gathered around a table in the back where we could get to know each other. Sue shared about their one month 'road trip' with the kids. Her mom had passed away just six months earlier, yet she had felt nudged by the Lord to have their entire family "Pray for a new Grandma! Pray that Grandpa will find someone who will love on all of you!" They prayed that prayer every day they were gone. They returned home to hear Don say, "I've found the woman I want to marry." They all gave us their blessings.

GOD ALWAYS GOES BEFORE US

We had one more important trip to make before we could set a wedding date! My first-born daughter, Shannon, and son-in-law, Steve, already knew a great deal about Don from his family. Plus our daily phone calls relayed a full description of everyone and everything in between! They were quite excited to see the fruits of their matchmaking in Southeast Asia. When we arrived in Atlanta, Don did not disappoint. My two grandsons and two granddaughters were thrilled with his attentive, conversational manner, interesting stories, and laughter. They thought Don a perfect match for me.

Don didn't want to miss out on the fun of finding a wedding dress for me, so he joined Shannon and me for our drive into Atlanta. We had set a tentative wedding date only three weeks away, so we knew we wouldn't have a big choice in dresses! We asked if they had any samples we could try. The first dress was

OUR WEDDING BY THE RIVER

perfect! A few alterations could be made in time and shipped to California for our family outdoor wedding in our yard along the Kings River. God is good! Steve, Shannon, and their kids all lived on a six acre farm in the beautiful countryside. It was idyllic and peaceful. We spent many hours getting acquainted, with great outdoor fun and indoor conversation around the fireplace.

The last evening in Atlanta, we went out for a family dinner. Don wanted Steve, Shannon, and the kids to be involved in asking my hand in marriage, making sure they were all in agreement. They all gave us their blessing. All that remained was to plan the wedding!

JOURNAL: 2005

"Oh Lord, you have placed your Hand upon me and Don Jackson to give us your abundant blessing and favor. I am so overwhelmed with Your love for us that I cry out with joy, Lord, that You have entrusted us with Your mantle of grace. Bless us always, Lord, with Your wisdom, discernment, guidance, and understanding as we bring our five families into one, under Your Holy Name, we pray. May our union as one glorify Your name. Amen."

We had the time of our lives planning the wedding. I told our five daughters they could plan "The Big Day." Tom, my daughter-in-law's father and a pastor, would officiate our marriage vows. The girls went online and ordered all the beautiful bridesmaid dresses, shoes, and accessories. The flowers came from a beautiful florist owned by Julie's in-law family. My niece-to-be, Susan, and friends planned all of the music and singing. Most all Jackson Family weddings are held on their own properties. With my family, there would now be 265 Jackson family members! Fortunately, nearly all had yards large enough for family gatherings.

Don and I wanted all our children, spouses, and all nineteen grandchildren (from sixteen years to nine months) to be in the wedding. The nine girls would wear white dresses, and the eight boys would sport khaki pants and white collared shirts. Our fourteen and sixteen-year-old granddaughters would be junior bridesmaids. Our daughters were all matrons of honor, dressed in beautiful California poppy orange-pink! Their spouses were all best men and the boys all best boys! We had more family in our wedding than we had guests. Inviting just the first two generations, we numbered about sixty!

All five families, both Don's and mine, were quite excited to finally meet. My daughters and their families arrived on Thursday evening prior to our Sunday wedding day. It was amazing to see them all gather for the first time. There was a "cousin" for everyone's age—sometimes four or five! The children all bonded immediately, happy to enlarge their respective family. There is only one answer for this: they were all believers in the Lord. My family was eager to have a Grandpa for their children and Don's family was eager to have a Grandma for their family—all to bless and to heal.

It was so much fun for the sisters-in-law to exchange sister gifts and share their excitement for all the last minute things to do—manicures and pedicures and pictures of every minute of every day. The guys all got acquainted and discussed plans for the ensuing days, taking tours around the ranches, playing volleyball, swimming, and driving my surrendered to the Lord, sea-mist-blue Jaguar convertible through the orchards for a closer look at all the fruit!

Now faith is the assurance of things hoped for,
the conviction of things not seen...

— *Hebrews 11:1*

HIS CONSECRATION : SHALL WE GATHER BY THE RIVER?

The bright-eyed sunny day was matched only by all our sunny, smiling faces as we set up tables, chairs, place settings, floral arrangements, and decorated each table with beautiful floral arrangements, oak leaves and Apple Pears.

The four o'clock wedding time meant we had all the time in the world to enjoy the preparations. Everyone saw a need and filled it, with children running around in clusters of activity, full of excitement and anticipation. Thanks to the orchestration of all the moms and dads, we all ended up ready at the same time!

Don and I had prearranged a time to meet down by the river for the mutual reveal prior to the wedding. I invited the little girls to walk down to the river with me for a sneak-peak of Grandpa in his white tux shirt, black jeans, and cowboy boots! It's one of my most precious memories of the day, seeing them run ahead of me. By the looks on their faces, you'd have thought they were marrying him! Such wonder, such love.

And I will restore the years the locusts have eaten.

— Joel 2:25

My two sons-in-law, Steve and Brandon, walked me down the "aisle" of grass, with rose petals strewn by the flower girls ahead of us. Fall had come to the river. Orange, yellow, and green lined the rivers edge, reflecting in the glassy water behind us. Surrounded by our five children, their spouses, our nineteen grandchildren, and our families, we exchanged our marriage vows down by the river between two hundred-year oak trees.

HIS ANOINTING : BY FAITH

By faith,   I had given up my "tree of security" in exchange for God's calling on my life. Had I not done so, I would not have been able to care for my four grandchildren while Steve and Shannon went to Southeast Asia with George and Colleen to "plan the meeting of Don and Jo."

By faith,   Don had built his house, praying the Lord would send him a wife.

By faith,   I had surrendered everything, so there was no going back. My path was set before me.

By faith,   Don and I had prayed daily for God's will to be done in our lives and the lives of our five families.

By faith,   Don had been the spiritual leader in bringing our families together, asking each couple for their blessing.

By faith,   We had placed our toes in the water of the riverbank of the Jordan River.

By faith,   We had heeded the call of God to bless and to heal our two families, who had been through so much, with His help and blessings.

By faith,   Don and I had crossed the river of grief to the Land of God's Promises!

Married with our matchmakers, George, Colleen, Shannon and Steve

Lest you think I exaggerated the details of our relationship, Don often adds even more memories when he tells the story of our seven-week, whirlwind romance. When he first came to my door, as he tells it, "It truly was love at first sight. Everything blended together when we heard each other's stories of loss and realized we both had children who were similar ages. I just knew God had brought us together. From the first day I met her, I knew it was going to work. I thank God every day that He loved us and saved us for each other."

After a time, Don yearned and prayed for the Lord to send him a wife, so he set about the task of building another house toward the front of the property on the river in Kingsburg. His thought was that if he built the house, God would provide the right woman to live there with him. He finished the house in April of 2005. Four months later, Don met me, Dear Reader, and you know the story from there.

We've told the story of our first dinner at the Montage Hotel overlooking the ocean many times in the years we've been married, and Don always adds, "I'll never forget sitting there with Jo, with the sun setting in the west with the big, round full moon coming up over the hills of Laguna! Never saw such a beautiful thing."

And that's what can happen when God's love, grace, and faithfulness writes your Love Story

The stream of God is full of water.

— *Psalm 65:9*

■ No matter where your life has brought you thus far, Dear Reader, I share the story above to give you encouragement and hope that Christ is the answer for everything in life. Never give up on Him and His plan for your life. Your story is not finished yet.

■ The blessings and favor the Lord is preparing for you will appear when you least expect them. He is working behind the scenes even when we don't see His Hand in our lives. Pray expectantly!

■ God not only gives us the desires of our heart, but also places those desires in our heart. He gives us the desire to want what He wants for us. Pay close attention to what the Lord places on your heart during your times of quiet and prayer with Him. Keep a journal close by to record these thoughts. We are very capable of making poor choices or bad decisions by not listening to God!

■ Waiting on the Lord develops our dependence on Him, so our lives are surrendered to His will, not ours.

■ Obedience takes center stage when God asks something of us we don't understand. We need to be obedient to His call, stepping out in faith, trusting in His guidance, goodness, and faithfulness.

■ God's miracles often come in silence, unannounced. Life is always an adventure with the Lord. Look for the small blessings in every day, the times the Lord answered a prayer, set a friend to call or stop by, etc. Nothing is a coincidence.

■ Let down your wings and feel God's love, calm, peace, and rest come into your heart. Let them down, be still, and listen in the quiet.

■ God loves a grateful heart. Reflect on the blessings and favor God has brought into your life up to now. Think of His spiritual blessings, His temporal mercies, His blessings of health, family, the joy of work, friendships, and the privilege of serving Him. They will restore your faith and fill you with "the joy of remembering."

Every good thing bestowed
    and every perfect gift is from above,
coming down from the Father of Lights,
    with Whom there is no variation,
no shifting shadow.

— *James 1:17*

STONE 11   GARLANDS OF GRACE

*O*ur hearts were filled with thankfulness to God for bringing Don and I together. We all lifted our arms to heaven and thanked God for all the blessings He was bestowing upon us by saying, "yes" and "thank you" to His blessing of each other. New life and new joy flowed into our families. A cloud had lifted and the sun was shining upon us all.

For my first harvest season, I learned how to drive Don's big pickup around the ranch, put on a pair of work boots and Oshkosh jeans, and even hiked myself up into the cab of a "semi" loaded with fruit, as he drove me from one end of the ranch to the other. We would collapse around midnight into the king bed in Don's RV, which still smelled like ammonia and Lysol from a heavy cleaning! Then we were up at dawn to begin a new day all over again. Don put me in charge of the women on the packing line, many of whom spoke little English. We smiled, giggled, and motioned to each other with our hands until we could communicate with words. They seemed happy to have "the boss's wife" working alongside of them. I was definitely a city girl in a farmer's fields—I mean orchards—of apricots, plums, peaches, and nectarines.

The first day I arrived at the packing shed, I was prepared to work! With my stash of work clothes in my bag, I drove the hour out to the ranch. Don and our son Steve, spotted me as I stepped out of our Mercedes wearing the Oshkosh bib jeans

given to me by my daughters, Shannon and Meghan at our wedding shower, white tennis shoes, large brim sun hat, and dark sunglasses.

Steve looked at me and laughed, "Well, Mom, I don't know if you'll be able to see the color of the fruit with those dark glasses on. And you won't need your hat, because we have you working in the shade all day!" I don't know who laughed harder, my husband, my son, or the ladies in the packing shed. I laughed along with them!

With 100 to 105 degree heat that first year, I only lasted four days before begging Don to let us go home for a strong shower and a good night's sleep in our own bed! I was a trooper, though, and helped with harvest season for the first four years. For the next three, however, I only drove out to check on everyone with trays of sandwiches!

HIS COMPASSION : ADJUSTMENTS TO THE BLESSINGS

Even with blessing and favor from the Lord, we found ourselves struggling to adjust to the changes. Coming to Kingsburg and leaving my life behind in southern California meant adjustments in all major areas—marriage, family, and friendships.

With Don leaving for the ranch at 5:30 in the morning and coming home at 5:30 at night, I suffered loneliness and feelings of isolation. Don had been widowed for twelve years, so adjustments for him were different. He was not accustomed to thinking of anyone else's schedules, desires, or needs. I could see he was also having a difficult time getting his boots back into the marriage saddle!

I remember my dismay one evening when I had spent hours preparing a great Pot Roast dinner for us one cold, wintery night. I was so excited for him to get home from the ranch, shower, and relax before dinner so we could talk about our day. Don came home, went into the bedroom to change—and came out an hour later. Dinner was well past done. I tried to conceal my disappointment as I served it. But when I sat down to pray with him, I was shocked to see his plate already clean! He had eaten the entire meal before I could sit down! I ran into the bedroom, crying.

I was displaced! I was discouraged! I wanted to go home!

MY FAMILY

Besides that, I missed my two daughters, sons-in-law, and my grandchildren! My daughters were also having difficulty with my lack of flexibility and availability. They were used to having me all to themselves, even though they loved and appreciated the fact that Don and three families had joined our circle. My daughter and two daughters-in-law in Kingsburg were all homeschooling their children five days a week from eight in the morning until two in the afternoon each day. Then they ran errands and kept up their households. Fortunately, weekends always brought us together with sports and family gatherings breaking up my loneliness during the week. I really appreciated my new daughter, Julie, calling me daily to see how things were going in our new lives.

The cultural adjustments to life in the San Joaquin Valley were also difficult for me. I missed the hustle and bustle of my hometown, with coffee places to meet, plenty of outdoor bistros for lunch, and an endless choice of restaurants and cultural activities for evenings and weekends. I had been a regular attendee with friends for Broadway, Opera, and Ballet at the Performing Arts Center. Plus, with my dad's passing in 2000, my stepmom and my three sisters were still an important part of my life. We celebrated birthday dinners together even though it meant traveling to each other's cities.

TREASURED FRIENDSHIPS

I had formed treasured friendships over the previous forty years. We had babies together, raised our children together, helped at church together, and attended Bible studies together. I missed my friends. I made the intentional decision to stay in touch with them, letting them know how important they were to me, no matter how often we saw each other.

I missed the clean air and ocean breezes and having my windows open every night without fear of bugs. It took me awhile to get used to closed windows and doors to keep out the dust, while keeping my fly swatter handy!

But more than anything, I missed hearing my name. There wasn't anywhere I could go in Newport Beach and Corona del Mar without seeing people I knew and who knew my name. No one but my family knew me in Kingsburg, although I loved hearing "Mom," and "Aunt Jo," and "Grandma!"

All of my underpinnings were gone, except Him. I knew only God could have taken me away from Orange County. I knew I was where He wanted me to be; nonetheless, it was difficult. I struggled with "fitting in" and finding my niche.

APRIL 26, 2008

"I'm learning when God calls us, it's not always easy to know how to respond. He has to equip us. One of the most difficult challenges of my new life here is the quiet, the isolation, the loneliness of not being around people, the withdrawal, as noted in today's devotion. 'Times of withdrawal for rest and learning always precede fresh work for My Kingdom. Be Still. Learn of Me.' I need to remember, this is from God, a time SET APART to BE with Him alone, to LEAN on Him alone, and LEARN of Him more."

When you make a vow to God,
do not delay in filling it.

— *Ecclesiastes 5:4*

FULFILLING MY VOW TO THE LORD

If you recall, I had made six promises to the Lord the night of my Surrender on the 55 Freeway. I had surrendered my Marriott career, my income, and security. I had surrendered my beloved One Ford Road house. I placed my house on the real estate sales market in December of 2005. It sold in three weeks. I had surrendered my Orange County, California lifestyle. I had surrendered California, but the Lord did not take that from me. I simply moved north to Kingsburg. I had surrendered my Lexus and had donated it to a ministry.

I had another promise to keep—the sale of my brand new, paid-in-full, sea-mist-blue, Jaguar convertible! I went to the local dealership two months after we were married and took a shellacking on it. My last and final vow to the Lord was to give him a tithe for all the money I had made over the past seven years! When my house sold that December, I kept my final promise to God: I mailed my tithe to a few of my favored ministries just hours before the year ended!

Believe me, there were many days I wanted to turn around and run home. I wanted to give up when I didn't want to face my weak self. I was so homesick. I missed my family, my friends, my home church, my grocery stores, and the Newport Beach Library! God had called me, this I knew. He had called for my total surrender before He gave me a new life. I could not dig up in doubt that which He had given me in faith.

There was no going back. There was nowhere to run. Kingsburg was now my home. Happily-ever-after doesn't always mean easily ever after! My surrender to Him required my persevering obedience to Him. "Do whatever you need to do, Jo, but don't give up! You are not a quitter!" I raised my arms to Heaven and said, "Yes!" and "Thank you, Lord!"

JOURNAL: Spring 2008

"Oh, Lord! You know my sadness, my feelings of isolation and loneliness, and my desire for friendship these past three years. I offer it all to you. Take me, make me, break me, mold me, as You are doing. I offer up to you my brokenness, my failures, my weaknesses, my unworthiness. Use me as You see fit. Transform my life dramatically in this my new life with Don, for ALL our children and ALL our grandchildren! I PRAY for the courage to give You my heart. Please, I beg You, mold it after Your own!"

HIS REFINING : EVERY STONE REQUIRES MAJOR GROWTH

For the first three years in Kingsburg, I filled my morning hours with quiet time with the Lord. I knew I had to dig deep into His Word. I wanted Him to re-define me in this new season. I needed His guidance to navigate this unfamiliar stone.

Now the LORD said to Abram,
"Go forth from your country,
And from your relatives
And from your father's house,
To the land which I will show you;
And I will make you a great nation,
And I will bless you,
And make your name great;
And so you shall be a blessing.

— Genesis 12:1-2

We can't move ahead while looking at what we've left behind. As my loving dad would have told me, "Pull up your bootstraps, Sweetie, and keep going!" I could feel my dad cheering me on from Heaven.

No one, having put his hand to the plow,
and looking back, is fit for the Kingdom of God.

— *Luke 9:62*

I could no longer afford to look back, I needed to keep going forward, pressing on, one step at a time. I would be about His Kingdom business. I promised God I would not look into the rearview mirror, but face and embrace His will for me:

- In my circumstances (my new home in Kingsburg)
- In my relationships (my husband, family, and friends)
- In my thinking (my plans and my potential taking root)
- In my commitments (to my husband, family, and friends)
- In my actions (how I live)
- In my beliefs (how I worship)

Don and I applied all we were learning on our journey into the blending of our two families. In time, with God's help, patience, and guidance, we completed the crossing of the Jordan River, setting our feet once again on solid ground, standing firmly on His faithfulness and blessings.

God gives us blessings for HIS purpose and HIS plans. We knew He wanted us to pass on these blessings to do His Kingdom work, to be alert and prepared to help others, to heal and serve others.

God took my identity and replaced it with His—to bless, heal, and serve others. He took my income and security and replaced it with financial means for Don and me to provide

Then Joshua called the twelve men from the people of Israel,
    who he had appointed, a man from each tribe.
And Joshua said to them, "Pass on before the ark of the LORD your God
    into the midst of the Jordan,
and take up each of you a stone upon his shoulder,
    according to the number of the tribes of the people of Israel,
that this may be a sign among you.
When your children (and grandchildren) ask in time to come,
    'What do these stones mean to you?'
then you shall tell them that the waters of the Jordan were cut off
    before the ark of the covenant of the LORD.
When it passed over the Jordan, the waters of the Jordan were cut off.
    So these stones shall be to the people of Israel a memorial forever.

— Joshua 4:4-7

You will be made rich in every way so that you can be generous on every occasion.

— 2 Corinthians 9:10-11

for children and the aged, the disabled, the poor, the unloved, and the lost. He took my empty home and replaced it with a home full of family, laughter, friendships, and fellowship.

As I think back to my Surrender on the 55 Freeway, I thank God for how He transformed my life. God has so richly blessed all of our family as a result of one act of sacrificial obedience. Never hesitate to surrender your all to God—He will richly reward those whose hearts are completely His.

HIS FAVOR : OUR GARLANDS OF GOD'S BLESSINGS

I will establish my covenant between me and you and your offspring after you throughout their generations for an everlasting covenant, to be God to you and to your offspring after you.

— Genesis 17:7

As I write these words, Don and I are celebrating the blessings of this season of life in full measure! In spite of all our failures and shortcomings, God has been faithful. When we were young, absorbed in our careers, busy with family demands, living with God on the back burner, God has been faithful! When we were going our own way, murmuring and complaining about our lives, living in disobedience, God has been faithful! In the midst of failed relationships and broken vows, He never let us go, never stopped pursuing us—the Faithful Hound of Heaven! Whether struggling to figure out how to live life or travailing the desert journeys of loss and grief, He has been faithful.

I encourage you to make "a forever-memorial," to tell your children and grandchildren that our faith needs to take our feet to the edge of the water, knowing God will always provide a way. It is good to celebrate His blessings. Celebration gives us hope for the future, filling our hearts with gratitude and thanksgiving. I encourage you to celebrate your children and grandchildren and great grandchildren! Your celebration may look differently for you than ours, but celebrate the good you see in members of your family. If your family is made of precious and close friends, celebrate them. Celebrating those you love will encourage and cultivate a legacy of generational blessing!

Pass on remembrances of what God has done in your life, what you have learned, what you hold dear, along with your favorite passages, verses, and stories in the Bible. Share who you are since Christ entered your life.

Then those who feared the Lord talked with each other,
and the Lord listened and heard.
A scroll of remembrance was written in His presence
concerning those who feared the Lord and honored His name.

— *Malachi 3:16*

HIS LEGACY : CELEBRATING OUR FAMILY

Dear Reader, I hope you will indulge me as I demonstrate what I mean by celebrating family. My hope is that this celebration of our Garlands of Grace will inspire you to celebrate yours. As you read the letters that follow to our children and grandchildren, think about your own family and how you might celebrate God's Expressions of Grace in and with them.

As I was with Moses, so I will be with you;

I will never leave you nor forsake you.

Be strong and courageous,

because you will lead these people to inherit

the land I swore to their forefathers to give them.

Be strong and very courageous.

Be careful to obey all the law my servant Moses gave you;

do not turn from it to the right or to the left,

that you may be successful wherever you go.

Do not let this Book of the Law depart from your mouth;

meditate on it day and night,

so that you may be careful to do everything written in it.

Then you will be prosperous and successful.

Have I not commanded you?

Be strong and courageous.

Do not be terrified; do not be discouraged,

for the Lord your God will be with you wherever you go.

—Joshua 1:5-9

Children are a heritage from the Lord, offspring a reward from Him.
Like arrows in the hands of a warrior are children born in one's youth.

— Psalm 127:3-4

TO OUR DEAREST CHILDREN

This letter is from both Dad and me,

even though I am writing it. We have both poured our love

and observations into this Epistle of Grace to you all. Our prayer is that it will

speak life into you now and long after we are gone. YOU are the Garlands of Grace

God blessed each Dad and I with when you were born.

For by grace you have been saved through faith.
And this is not our own doing, it is the gift of God,
not a result of works, so no one may boast.

— Ephesians 2:8-9

There is a quietness that touches each of us when we are in the presence of
God, and the Holy Spirit touches us. We become more spiritual, humble, at peace
in His will, and more confident in our way. We witness this in all of you, our dear
children, whenever we are with you. Dad and I would like to share the blessed
Expressions of Grace we see in you, your marriages, and in your families.

You all began your married life with the love of the Lord in your hearts. Men,
the greatest gift you've given your children is loving their mother. Dad and I are so
grateful for how you love and cherish your wives. We encourage each of you to love
your wife beyond measure, to treasure her, and to make your relationship with her
a priority. Say you're sorry. Ask forgiveness. Be the spiritual head of your family.

You all began early with your children (our grandchildren!) in Growing Them

God's Way, cultivating and shepherding your children's hearts for God. Dad and I love seeing how you have modeled a spiritual life of prayer, teaching them that God loves them and has a plan for their lives, and showing them abundant amounts of God's grace and love. You welcome the Holy Spirit into your lives each day, preparing your hearts to be open to His guidance. You work together, intentionally parenting and putting prayerful, deliberate thought into guiding each child's life with the help of the Holy Spirit. Being intentional to invest in their lives has provided a safe haven in which to grow their character, strengthening their spiritual and moral qualities, distinctive with a life lived for Christ.

Each of you is blessed with a keen sense of observation to see the unique giftedness the Lord has given to each of your children. You all sacrifice to ensure you are giving them opportunities to discover, learn, and grow in their giftedness. As parents, you invest time and energy, placing the needs of each child ahead of your own, teaching and training to desire and value hard work, diligence, and perseverance to obtain their goals. We love seeing you pour into and interact with our grandchildren.

You are engaged and influential in the friends they make and the company they keep, creating a welcoming home that encourages everyone into their lives. You teach the value of relational living, by honoring, respecting, and celebrating family time with love and laughter. You are always available to them, strengthening their value and worth.

You are also raising them to be amazing husbands and wives to the spouses we have all been praying for these many years! (The one daughter and two sons of yours who are already married have embraced the marriage role with seriousness and dedication.)

Moms, you have not only been teaching your daughters to organize a home,

Do not grow weary in doing good.

— 2 Thessalonians 3:13

plan, shop, cook, decorate, and throw the best gatherings ever—all while taking care that every detail be warm and welcoming to each and every guest, but you are also preparing both your sons and daughters in guiding, training, and educating each of them for expressing and pursuing their passions, while aspiring for academic and humanitarian endeavors and doing it with excellence.

Dads, you have been teaching them to appreciate hard work and to be responsible for themselves. You're teaching them to provide for and support their families and provide the skills they'll need to sustain them in their adult lives in whatever profession God has called them. You work tirelessly and sacrificially to provide the means for them to pursue their goals, helping when needed. With your sons and daughters, you make and take the time for fun and recreation doing your favorite things together.

You ALL are so involved in all areas of raising your children. We are so proud and grateful for each one of you. As encouragers, our dear children, you speak life and blessing into our grandchildren, giving them God's world-perspective on life. We love how you teach them love and respect for other adult family members, especially their aunts, uncles, and grandparents! This effort, by the way, will come back to you extravagantly!

You live your lives blessed by the fruit of the Spirit: love, joy, peace, patience, kindness, goodness, faithfulness, gentleness, and self-control. We see these fruits of the Spirit in each of you, whenever we are with you.

You make life fun, and it is a blessing to be around you! We love all of our gatherings, large or small—although they're usually large! Every special occasion is always wonderful, because we celebrate our common good—not our differences— and our love for one another and not ourselves.

Your walk with the Lord will not make you weary;
it will invigorate you, restore your strength,
and energize your life.

— Matthew 11:28-29

Our treasured children, all ten of you, Dad and I simply can't speak enough about the love, admiration, and respect we have for each and every one of you. We thank God for you, by name, each and every day in prayer, grateful beyond measure for the gracious blessings He has given you and us.

Dad and I each thank you for taking us into your families and adopting us as "Dad" and "Mom," and "Grandpa" and "Grandma." That single decision has made all the difference in the world as we have "Come Together as One." Each of us, respectively, loves you as our very own.

Thank you for being "the best" of us, for loving us, blessing us, keeping us young at heart, and living your life with excellence with God's grace!

With all our love, devotion, and continued prayers,

Dad and Mom

XOXO

And in their prayers for you their hearts will go out to you,
because of the surpassing grace God has given you.
Thanks be to God for His indescribable gift!

— 2 Corinthians 9:14

BLUE RIBBON DAY

FAMILY MEMORY IN EMERALD BAY

TO OUR DEAREST GRANDCHILDREN

It's time for "A Gathering of All Our Grandchildren," so Grandpa and I can celebrate you and the Expressions of God's Grace we see in each of you! God has, indeed, blessed all of us by bringing us together in His divine plan to spend the rest of our earthly days and eternity together.

Grandma's family was without a Grandpa. Grandpa's family was without a Grandma. God looked down and saw two people who had a lot of love in their hearts for God, their children, and their grandchildren. He sent Uncle George and Aunt Colleen, and Uncle Steve and Aunt Shannon on a trip with Ravi Zacharias to Southeast Asia—and the rest is the Lord's love story as I shared in Stone 10.

Grandpa and I are proud, exceedingly happy, and blessed to now have twenty-two grandchildren with our combined families! We also already have been blessed with two adorable great-grandchildren! Can you imagine what's going to happen when all of you are getting married and having babies! Grandpa and I will hardly be able to keep up with all their names, but we will still be praying for each and every one of you, by name, each and every day!

Because there are twelve stones in this story of God's faithfulness, we chose twelve Expressions of God's Grace we collectively see in you. Please keep in mind as you read, all of you have several of these expressions of grace within you. You will recognize yourself when you read the descriptions. When Grandpa and I are with you, we are amazed at how God is working within you, molding your gifts and natural talents for His Kingdom.

Thus, these expressions of God's grace in you are intertwined with your gifts and talents. We have not listed them by importance or value. Each expression of God's grace upon you is very, very special.

GRACE OF ADVENTURE

Most all of you have been born with a sense of adventure burning within you. You love to travel and see new lands, countries, and people. Many of you, who are old enough, have been on missions of God's love more than once. Many of you have traveled with your Mom and Dad as they have introduced you to cultures different than our own. All of these adventures have given you an understanding and compassion for others. You have sung with them, worshipped with them, spoken God's love to them, held them, hugged them, and cried for them. You have used your gifts of mercy, teaching, and serving others to show the love of Christ.

In addition, you've gained an understanding of and appreciation for the freedoms and opportunities we have in our own country. Grandpa and I pray you will continue to travel extensively and bring Christ's love to a hurting world.

GRACE OF CHARISMA & PERFORMANCE

All of you exhibit this combination in one form or another! Grandpa and I see it in all of you, no matter the age. Charisma is having a presence about you, showing others you are engaged and interested in what they are saying or doing. When you give attentiveness to people, they trust you and are drawn into your presence.

We see your poise and self-confidence as it continues to grow in you, because of the wide range of experiences our families pursue. When you are sharing your goals, passions, and dreams, you all come alive. Your faces light up and people are drawn into your compelling inspiration.

WEDDING DAY

ANTICIPATION

Being able to converse with anyone, of any age, anywhere is a honed ability that shows you care. Many of you are more mature on your life journey, investing time, commitment, dedication, and training to your goals and passions, whether in leadership, technology, business, farming, dance, sport, or healing and care-giving. And we applaud you for it!

GRACE OF CREATIVITY & IMAGINATION

Every area of life requires creativity and imagination. Sharing your artistry with others is a gift from God that we engage as his sub-creators. God blessed us with the ability to be creative and tend to the rich world HE created for us to enjoy. That is why discovering your unique strengths, gifts, and talents is so important. Keep in mind some of your gifts may not be revealed until God gives you an assignment!

We have quite a few creative entrepreneurs in our family, to say the least—several, in fact, in every family! We love to see your initiative and innovative resourcefulness in problem solving and delivering value to others. Never underestimate the value of having a vision or dream no one else can see and the commitment and perseverance to carry it out.

GRACE OF GRATITUDE & FORGIVENESS

This is a grace from God so many of you exhibit fully, while your younger cousins are learning, honing the skill of a thankful heart. All of your parents possess this grace and willingly share it with you. It is being thankful, recognizing the many blessings God gives you each day. Last week, one of our pastors asked, "If you woke up tomorrow morning possessing only what you thanked God for today, what would you have?"

We find it so appealing in you when you are softhearted, merciful and understanding of others. You quickly, freely, and fully forgive others—a rare thing in this world. Keep on being grateful for everyone and everything and being forgiving in all ways! You will sleep easier at night and permit others to rest in the grace you show.

GRACE OF STRENGTH & RESOLUTION OF HEART

This grace may sound a bit wordy, but it's stronger than gratitude and forgiveness and more encompassing than heart alone. Grandpa and I see this grace within you that comes from the Holy Spirit. There is a passion of expectancy, eagerness, and anticipation emanating from you as you look for your divine appointments each day. As a result, you are willing and prepared to extend kindness and courtesy to others. It is a big part of the gift of leadership you possess, which we will discuss below. You are willing to serve, to sit in the last row, to be humble in your evaluation of self.

There is a quiet, but strong and resolute tenderness about you that I call "My Quiet, Gentle Giant." (I'm referring to both Granddaughters and Grandsons here.) You are the one everyone can rely on to be there when the going gets tough—what a gift!

"Beginning today,

treat everyone you meet

as if they were

going to be dead

by midnight.

Extend to them

all the care, kindness,

and understanding

you can muster,

and do it with no

thought of any reward.

Your life will never

be the same again."

—Og Mandino

"Kind words can be short and easy to speak

but their echoes are truly endless."

— Mother Teresa

GRACE OF HEALER & RESTORER

We chose this grace to address patience, listening, thoughtfulness, caring, being a kind and tender healer and a restorer of good health. At the time of this writing, two of you are in the medical field, with another declaring Pre-Med. We are so grateful for this call and anointing the Lord has placed on your lives. There are several more of you aspiring to the medical field as well, whether in nursing or surgical professions. Some of you will seek advanced degrees for hospital clinical work or in research and teaching in university settings.

We have no doubt that several of you will lead others in the agricultural, business and political realms to heal our land and restore our way of life. May you do so with integrity and esteem for others, sharing your vision and passion. We encourage you to seek the Lord's will in every endeavor. He will direct you with His calling on your heart.

GRACE OF INTELLIGENCE, HUMOR, & LAUGHTER

You may all stand up on this one! It's why we have so much fun together! We "get" one another! You are all "learners", always acquiring more information and skills through experience and education. While you all are intelligent, some are wired to be intellectuals—forever students of intellectual thought and challenging conversations.

All of you have the grace of humor and laughter. When Grandpa and I are with you, you delight us with your display of great wit and acumen. There's always such humor and laughter when we are with you in every setting. You are conversational, funny, insightful, and wise. It's always great to have a cheerful heart and laugh with family and friends. Laughter is an amazing gift of grace from God and some of the best medicine anyone could ever give!

"Humor is the salt of personality.
Its presence is an evidence of good nature,
of an appreciation of the real values of life....
It is the most effective means of easing a difficult situation.
Here it is important to differentiate between wit and humor:
wit is of the mind, humor is of the heart."

— Charles Gow

"Humor is the harmony of the heart."

— Douglas Jerrold

SUMMER DAYS

GRACE OF INDEPENDENCE

This grace is subtler than most, because it is seen in your unspoken self-confidence and self-sufficiency. It is not independence from family, but rather self-reliance and resourcefulness! Through years of encouragement and affirmations, your parents have been fostering your sense of autonomy and ability to stand on your own.

GRACE OF LEADERSHIP

We are not speaking here of the spiritual gift of leadership, although that may also be true, but rather the intentional, acquired skills of leadership with a heart tuned to God. You are the ones who are salt and light to those around you, always putting your best foot forward. It's being a friend to everyone, being inclusive of their thoughts and contributions of thought or ideas. It's having a knack for getting along with people, with an open mind and head that stays clear under stress.

What leaders come to mind when you read these eleven attributes of leadership from Napoleon Hill?

1. *Unwavering courage.*
2. *Self-control.*
3. *A keen sense of justice.*
4. *Definiteness of decision.*
5. *Definiteness of plans.*
6. *The habit of doing more than paid for.*
7. *A pleasing personality.*
8. *Sympathy and understanding.*
9. *Mastery of detail.*
10. *Willingness to assume full responsibility.*
11. *Cooperation.*

"There are many

who have lost

the opportunity

for success because

they have given up

too soon. Perseverance

is a key to victory."

— Jaime Garrido

You might begin by thanking your parents for exhibiting and passing on these qualities to you...

GRACE OF PERSEVERANCE

You've heard of the value of perseverance since early in your schooling years; you've read it in Scripture. We must allow the Scriptures to strengthen us to press on in the race marked out for us. You have faced strong competition in your sports and academic environments. You have shown determination and endurance when the going gets tough, whether accomplishing a personal goal, or working along side other team members to achieve victories or reach academic goals.

Races test endurance. You all possess it deep in your DNA! Staying power, tenacity, and true grit will take you to the finish line. We have seen this in you within the defining moment when it is you alone with yourself, stretching for the finish line or to beat the clock. You are all winners in perseverance.

GRACE OF CHARACTER & MORAL COURAGE

"Character develops

itself in the stream of life."

— Johann Wolfgang
von Goethe

You all exhibit character! Those of you who are younger siblings will have great examples to follow with your older sisters, brothers, and cousins, as well as continued guidance from your Dad and Mom.

We are especially proud of each of you for your strength of character and moral courage. Grandpa and I have witnessed numerous times your loyalty to a friend, teacher, or family member when they have been misunderstood or needed someone to stand up for them. You have shown trustworthiness in your relationships with others, especially your parents.

Each in your family units has preserved the good name and character of your family's reputation.

ACCOMPLISHED

PROUD GRANDPARENTS

A good name is to be chosen rather than great riches.

— Proverbs 22:1

We know many (or all) of you have experienced lies said by others, the painful betrayal of friends, hurtful slander and gossip, and those who talk behind your back. Yet you show a smile when you see them and turn the other cheek to preserve your honor. In some cases, you have gone to them privately to resolve the conflict. Grandpa and I have been so proud of the way you've shown moral strength in a conflict. As believers, we are to be imitators of God and walk by the Spirit. Even if we are slandered, we are to do good. This is one of my favorite Scriptures:

Whatever is true, whatever is honorable, whatever is just,
whatever is pure, whatever is lovely, whatever is commendable;
if there is any excellence, if there is anything worthy of praise,
think about these things.

— Philippians 4:8

You have shown fortitude (courage) and moral strength in how you've responded to betrayals or challenges to conform to another's thoughts and actions. There have been times when you have been attacked to the very core of your beliefs. At times, good moral courage means you simply walk away. May you continue to be brave and courageous men of valor and women of virtue.

GRACE OF WISDOM

The fear of the Lord is the beginning of all wisdom;
all who follow His precepts have good understanding.

— **Psalm 111:10**

Wisdom is supreme; therefore, get wisdom.
Though it cost all you have, get understanding.
Esteem her and she will exalt you, embrace her, she will honor you.
She will set a garland of grace on your head
and present you with a crown of splendor.

— **Proverbs 4:7**

Grandpa and I see this grace of wisdom unfolding for each of you as you have been growing and maturing, making good use of your knowledge of this beautiful grace God will freely give to all of you.

With humility comes wisdom"

— **Prov.11:2**

I see this as especially true for those of you who are more mature. You seek the virtue of humility, which we all pray for, lassoing the prideful natures within all of us. All of you, clothe yourselves with humility toward one another.

God opposes the proud but gives grace to the humble.

— **I Peter 5:5**

UNFORGETTABLE DAYS

FAMILY TIMES

Do nothing out of selfish ambition or vain conceit,
but in humility consider others better than yourselves.

— **Philippians 2:3**

The wisdom that comes from heaven is first of all pure;
then peace-loving, considerate, submissive,
full of mercy and good fruit, impartial and sincere.
Peacemakers who sow in peace raise a harvest of righteousness.

— *James 3:17-18*

Oh, dear Grandes, seek and pray for wisdom. God freely gives it, if we but ask. Grandpa and I pray daily for wisdom as we pray for each of you. May you all continue to use good judgment and discernment, as you have in your lives thus far, to make the more consequential, major decisions you'll face as you grow older. All of your parents are wise! Do not hesitate to seek their advice. Grandpa and I are always here for you, too. And our prayers for wisdom for all of you will continue long after we are gone!

Tell it to your children and let your children tell it to their children,
and their children to the next generation.

— *Joel 1:3*

For all of you older siblings and cousins, we urge you to help the little ones. They all look up to you as their big brothers, sisters, and cousins to help show them the way. Reach out to them and pay attention, especially to those who may not

reach out to you but need the attention and guidance you can give. They are watching how you live with strength of character and perseverance.

In conclusion, our precious Grandchildren, be strong and courageous! It is up to YOU to lead your generation and the next generation into God's land of promise, teaching about God's faithfulness, God's power, and God's love! God uses the younger generation of faithful men and women to carry on His work in the Lord.

You are loved, valued, and special beyond words. Grandpa and I will be praying for each of you, by name, every day. May our support and unconditional love empower you, with God's help, toward maturity. May our words of affirmation strengthen you, encourage you, lift you to a life lived with Him and filled with blessings for your bright future.

What we do with our lives is important—how we spend our time, what we neglect, what priorities we set, what attitudes we project, and the goals we set and achieve.

Always say:

- *Please*
- *Thank You*
- *Excuse Me*
- *I'm Sorry*
- *Forgive Me*
- *May I Help You?*
- *I Appreciate You*
- *I Love You!*

(I just had to throw those in!)

My dear grandchildren, how you have touched Grandpa and I with your love! You have moved us in ways that touch us deeply and give us such a swelling of gratitude and thanksgiving. You inspire us daily. You reinforce our Faith. I have shared the

FUTURE LEADERS

OUR GREAT GRANDCHILDREN

following Scripture with you all at one time or another. It has been and continues to be my daily prayer for each of you as you grow and navigate your own stones in the river.

So, my dear Grandchildren, when your children and grandchildren seek an answer for the meaning of your stones in the river, tell them your stories, your failings, your loss and grief, the hard places you persevered and never gave up. Teach them to your children, recognizing, celebrating, and enjoying the garlands of God's grace and blessing blossoming through them!

Because through it all, God is faithful.

Grandpa and I have no greater joy than our children and grandchildren walking with the Lord. (3 John 4). And now, our dear ones, may

The Lord bless you and keep you;

May the Lord make his face shine upon you, and be gracious to you;

May the Lord turn His face toward you, And give you peace.

—Numbers 6:24-26

God's blessings to all of you, our precious Grandchildren, Great-grandchildren, and all future generations to come. You will always be in our hearts. We love you to the ends of the earth and will be cheering and welcoming you as, one day, you join us to be together forever in Heaven.

Grandpa and Grandma (Grammie)
Poppi and Gigi
XOXOXOXOXOXOXOXOXOXO

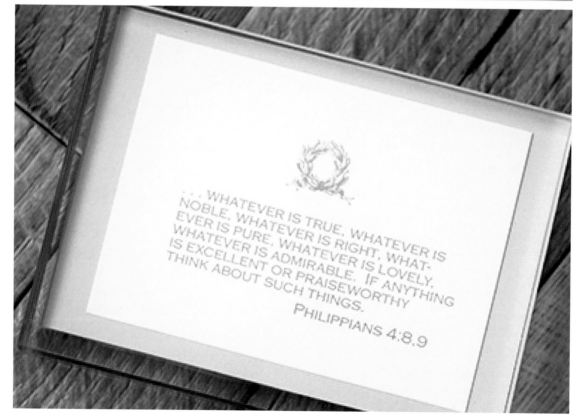

. . . WHATEVER IS TRUE, WHATEVER IS
NOBLE, WHATEVER IS RIGHT, WHAT-
EVER IS PURE, WHATEVER IS LOVELY,
WHATEVER IS ADMIRABLE, IF ANYTHING
IS EXCELLENT OR PRAISEWORTHY
THINK ABOUT SUCH THINGS.

PHILIPPIANS 4:8,9

GRACE NOTES | *Garlands of Grace*

- Don't dig up in doubt that which God has given you in faith! Trust the Lord's calling. He may not make the details clear to you. Take the next step, knowing He is going before you and want's your faith in following him. Stay faithful and continue on until blessings bloom!

- When God calls us, it is not always easy to know how to respond. He has to equip us. Pray for His equipping.

- If our view is a worldly perspective, we are apt to think His blessings are for us, but our blessings are to be used for His Kingdom purposes. Think with a heavenly perspective of how you can give it away. Pay it forward and, sometimes, pay it back.

- In each season and stone, there is still the journey with Him. Imagine staking a flag in the ground, declaring, "This ground right here now is Holy ground, already conquered in Christ." Celebrate the joy and give praise to Him for His glory.

- Write a letter to your children, recognizing in them the garlands of grace and blessing they have given to you through Christ.

- Write a letter to your grandchildren, celebrating the expressions of grace you see exhibited in them. They will read this love letter long after you are gone.

As you come to him,
    a living stone rejected by men
but in the sight of God
    chosen and precious.

—1 Peter 2:4

STONE 12   A FRESH CALLING

*H*ave you ever asked yourself what your life would have been like had you not answered God's call? I have. When I was a high school senior, Miss Hamilton, my counselor, strongly suggested my aptitude was for a Teaching career.

"But I'd like to be a nurse," I answered.

"Yes, Joanne, but all of your testing shows you would make a wonderful teacher." I pushed back. "My heart is really more like Cherry Ames, Student Nurse (a popular book series for girls in the 1940s-50s). I love to help sick people. I think I'd make a better nurse."

Despite my protests, Miss Hamilton won. I enrolled in the University of Wisconsin in Madison, as an English major with an Education minor. When I moved to California, I completed my undergraduate degree and California teaching credential and taught school for four years before having children, then taught Lamaze childbirth classes for four years. Yet I never lost my heart for nursing.

God's fingerprints were on my calling "to bless and to heal." I didn't need to be in a hospital to give God's blessings and grace of healing to those I met. Not until later, when God called me to be a wife and a mother, did I see He had already prepared me with teaching and nursing skills that would serve me well in motherhood!

As a young mom, I was aware of God's hand on my life and that of my family. I often read God's command to Joshua to build a monument off the banks of the Jordan

River that would remind the people of God's awesome power. I promised myself to build a similar tower of rocks in our backyard, a visual testimony to our daughters of all the times God had been faithful in our lives. But I never got around to it. So when my "fresh calling" came to write this book about God's faithfulness, Stones in the River was the title that immediately came to mind.

HIS INSTRUCTION : GOD PREPARES THOSE HE CALLS

The seeds of this book began long ago. When one daughter was married and our younger daughter was about to graduate high school, I prayed to write and speak to women. I knew the Lord was impressing this work on my heart. With a few speaking assignments under my belt, I thought my time was near. But then my husband was diagnosed with tongue cancer in 1995, and my calling as a caregiver continued for seven years.

One morning in my quiet time with the Lord a few months later, I felt His encouragement as I prayed for other women who were feeling isolated and alone, as I was.

"I will give you the words, Jo, and teach you what to say. Trust Me." I did not know what those words meant at the time but wrote them in the margin of my Bible nonetheless. At that time, I was a sales team leader at Newport Coast Villas, which qualified me to train, equip and motivate our sales team at our daily 8:00 a.m. meetings. Being newly widowed, I was eager to share real life with my younger sales team. I began weaving stories into our meetings. As they sipped their morning cups of coffee, I told my stories, teaching Godly values, character-building, and the importance of being others-centered. The team members often came to me privately, asking me to write the stories down or to share other lessons of life.

When I began The Master's Program for Women two years later, finding my calling "To Bless and To Heal" set me on my path for His Kingdom work. I asked the Lord to give me a big Kingdom assignment and writing was always at the forefront of my prayer.

After the Lord blessed me with Don Jackson, brought me to Kingsburg, and joined our two amazing families, I watched Him bring blessing and healing to each of our families who had experienced great loss. As I sought the Lord's guidance each and every morning, He gave me endless hours with Him in the early hours after Don left for the ranch—preparing me, guiding me, and filling me with His Truths. I stayed in touch with my prayer sisters and other godly women in my life, my mentors and teachers of His Word.

We began our married life in Kingsburg in October, and by spring I had made two discouraging discoveries: none of my favorite southern flowers bloomed in the north! More importantly, I discovered I wasn't doing such a great job of adapting to my new soil in my new environment, either! But God was such a faithful Gardener; He watered me with His Living Waters, fertilized me with His Word, and tenderly cared for me like a little shoot. He promised me I would bloom where He had planted me. In turn, I promised Him I would be faithful and trust in Him.

I will restore the years the locusts have eaten.

— Joel 2:25

BIBLE MARGIN: *April 26, 2007*
I'm learning when God calls us it is not always easy to respond. What are you calling me to, Lord? He whispers, "Be still and learn of Me."

His Holy Spirit guides us to pray
according to God's will.

—Romans 8:26-28

Though life was busy and full with our now-combined family, I once again found myself in a time of waiting. Dear Reader, you've probably noticed the pattern by now: God regularly takes us aside to teach and prepare, equipping us for His purpose and plan for our lives.

God gives you the desire to do His will.

— *Philippians 2:13*

I had prayed to write a book for years, but God had never revealed if or what that would look like. Taking me from Newport Beach to Kingsburg had indeed enlarged my territory and given me a God-sized assignment. What would God have me do with all this learning and preparation? I didn't have the answer; I only knew that life with Him is always an adventure!

Twelve women shared this journey with me: my teaching leader, Sandy, and the eleven women of our Master's class. For three years we had met quarterly, each of us seeking a Kingdom calling for our lives. As part of Graduation, each woman read a prepared paper of what she had learned in the three-year study regarding personal, family, and Kingdom realms. The teaching leader, in turn, read a prepared statement of what she observed in each of us

I share here what Sandy shared about me that evening, March 14, 2007. As you read it, think of how the Lord is preparing you for His fresh calling for you.

Jo, God has challenged you with a new life in this season. Walk in courage and knowledge that He has already given you all that you will need to serve Him. He knows the calling He has for you, and when

He reveals it, you will realize that you have already been prepared for it. Your time is coming. Remain faithful in this time of waiting and do not be discouraged.

So I waited and prepared. It's true; we never know when the call will come.

HIS TIMING : ALERTED TO THE CALL

Mine came three years later in 2010, during my quiet time: "Write the book of My faithfulness." Six words—that was it! As I did my chores that morning, I walked around the house repeating those six words and wondering, What do they mean?

The Lord had blessed Don and me by bringing us together, along with our married children and grandchildren. Perhaps He wanted me to write about our love story, which He had so clearly ordained! It was certainly proof of His faithfulness. My husband was not quite so enthusiastic about the time writing a book might require. He knew several authors who used ghostwriters to write their books for that very reason. But I was not at all convinced the Lord wanted me to pass on my calling to someone else!

One day, after several conversations about this, a friend gave me the name of a ghostwriter in San Diego. As I walked to my car, name in hand, I felt the Holy Spirit softly calming me, "Jo, I AM your ghostwriter."

The Lord had already prepared Don's heart by the time I shared this with him at dinner. He not only understood but also gave his blessing to me of the time, discipline, and obedience it would demand of both of us to meet this call from God. That night, we placed it all at His feet and pledged to work together to make it happen. "It will be fun to tell the Lord's love story for our children and grandchildren!" Little did we know what He had in mind!

JOURNAL: November 10, 2010

Mark this day as the day I begin writing, being OBEDIENT to the HOLY SPIRIT to 'write the book of God's faithfulness.' I have NO IDEA what that looks like yet, but I'm naming it Stones in the River, relating to God's faithfulness, based on the Book of Joshua, chapters 1-7. Please confirm your call to me, Lord.

PUTTING ON THE CALL

It didn't take long for God to reveal He had something far different planned for His book of faithfulness than anything I had ever dreamed. As a longtime reader of Stephen Covey, I like to "begin with the end in mind." Thus, it was most perplexing and frustrating for me not to have a clear picture of what the finished book would contain, let alone what it would look like! As I prepared for this assignment, however, stone after stone began to come to mind. God had, indeed, called me to an assignment I could not do without Him! One of my Master's Teachers, Rochelle, encouraged me: "The Lord has given you a pen, Jo, and He wants you to use it, so you need to write! If you're not obedient, He'll find someone else to do it!"

Further confirmation came from our pastor, answering all my questions of fear and doubt. As though speaking directly to me, he challenged us at the start of the new year "not to despise small beginnings." He continued, "Faithfulness with little leads to faithfulness with much. God's Word to us is not to be based on the opinions or viewpoints of other people. When He gives us an order, we need to grab hold of it as a guarantee that it will be! What will be the verb of your obedience? "Write it down!"

I wrote in my journal, *"To Teach and To Write!"*

Our pastor continued to draw a parallel to the very passage shaping my book:

"Our faith needs to take our feet to the edge of the water, knowing our God will prepare a way and equip us! Step into the Jordan! Don't avoid it with walls and obstacles! Circle it with praise and adoration to God! Like Jericho, the walls will come down!"

Confirmation if ever I'd heard it! I began gathering my stones, writing things down while I waited, praying and growing closer to Him.

BIBLE MARGIN: March 28, 2012

"Lord, I feel your pleasure when I write, Your Presence and Your Blessing."

My faith increased as I waited for God to show me the next step. I began arranging my days around Him and His calling. Alongside my quiet time, study, prayer, and reading of His Word, I wrote ideas on index cards, filing them in a large accordion file. I was gathering my stones. I stepped out in faith, asking prayer from family and prayer warriors in our lives. I sought the guidance of my prayer sisters and spiritual mentors, some of whom had authored books of their own. One of them cautioned me, "If your book is all fluff and phoniness, no one will read it, so make it transparent and real to give God's hope and encouragement to all who read it."

Prayer friends began sending me Scripture to affirm and support my writing. Almost every day, my Bible reading or devotional offered words regarding my desire "to bless and to heal." I put on His call in a leap of faith and a conscious, serious commitment. I thanked Him for this fresh calling for my life, filled with excitement for this assignment!

So teach us to number our days,
that we may present to Thee
a heart of wisdom.

— **Psalm 90:12**

For I know the plans that I have for you, 'declares the Lord,
  'plans for welfare and not for calamity to give you a future and a hope.
Then you will call upon Me and come and pray to Me, and I will listen to you.
    And you will seek Me and find Me, when you search for Me with all your heart.
And I will be found by you, 'declares the Lord,' and I will restore your fortunes
    and will gather you from all the nations
and from all the places where I have driven you, 'declares the Lord,
    'and I will bring you back from the place I sent you into exile.'

    — Jeremiah 29:11-14

At the same time, I still battled doubt and fear that I had mistaken His call or that I was unqualified. Then a prayer sister reminded me: "He doesn't call the equipped; He equips the called. Delayed obedience is disobedience!" I doubled down in prayer for wisdom and knowledge, discipline and obedience! I prayed for the Holy Spirit to be my guide with every written word. I prayed to use my time and His wisdom to make a difference in the lives of my children and grandchildren who would hold this book in their hands someday and read of God's faithfulness.

HIS TRUTH : PRAYING FOR WISDOM

I once heard it said, "Wisdom is the ability to apply God's truths to our daily lives." God has marked out your journey in your stones in the river, Dear Reader. As you look back and understand your journey, seeing the mosaic pattern of your stones, you gain more understanding of God's wisdom. As you go through this process yourself, seek God's guidance. Pray for wisdom. He promises to give it liberally (James 1:5).

My child, listen to what I say, and treasure my commands.
Tune your ears to wisdom, and concentrate on understanding.
Cry out for insight, and ask for understanding.
Search for them as you would for silver; seek them like hidden treasures.
Then you will understand what it means to fear the Lord,
and you will gain knowledge of God. For the Lord grants wisdom!
From his mouth come knowledge and understanding.

— Proverbs 2:1-6

What is the most important thing God wants from us? He has chosen us and set us apart to be men and women after God's own heart. The older we get, the more we realize our need to depend on God. The heart is what matters; our goal must be to satisfy God with a beautiful heart! From our heart, we will love and obey Him and proclaim His faithfulness.

Right now, you may feel God has forgotten you and left you without a mission. But God is faithful! He will not leave you where you are! Indeed, He may be preparing you for a new beginning, a fresh calling with Himself at the center. Trust the Truth of your calling. Have faith there is still a calling on your life. He who has called you will see it come to fruition.

The One Who calls you is faithful and He will do it with us and in us.

— 1 Thessalonians 5:24

Stay in conversation with God, wanting to grow closer, to learn Who He is. Bring your requests to Him with faith and belief to back them up! Pray the secret desires of your heart, asking for His confirmation. Pray with thanksgiving and praise for all God has blessed you with in your life so far. Worship Him with all your heart.

HIS COUNSEL : LEARNING TO LISTEN

How do we recognize God's call? How do we know His voice? We first look to where He has already spoken—His written Word divinely inspired by the Holy Spirit speaking through His prophets and disciples—the Bible. If we desire to hear God's voice, we must be familiar with His Word, for He never contradicts His written revelation in the Bible.

Prepare your heart each day before you open His Word. Ask the Holy Spirit to reveal God's truth to you, to hear His voice deep within your spirit. Reading God's Holy Word washes our minds of daily stress and clears out worry. It paves the way for our inner spirit to develop relationship with God the Father, Jesus the Son, and the Holy Spirit.

Whoever is of God hears the words of God.
The reason why you do not hear them
is that you are not of God.

— *John 8:47*

I AM the good shepherd. I know my own and my own know me,
just as the Father knows me and I know the Father;
and I lay down my life for my sheep.

— *John 10:14-15*

My sheep hear my voice, and I know them, and they follow me.
I will give them eternal life, and they will never perish,
and no one will snatch them out of my hand. My Father,
who has given them to me, is greater than all,
and no one is able to snatch them out of the Father's hand.
I and the Father are one.

— *John 10-27-28*

Cultivate a heart that listens. Be silent and still. We who belong to God hear what He says. He knows our thoughts, our fears, our deep longings. We can trust He will never take us where it isn't safe to go. He guides and teaches us His way. He sets the stones in our river to teach us, train us, and grow us into fully mature women of God. The more time you spend listening to God as you read the Bible, the closer you will become with Him.

Call to Me and I will answer you,
and will tell you great and hidden things
that you have not known.

— Jeremiah 33:3

I will instruct you and teach you in the way you should go;
I will counsel you with My eye upon you.

— Psalm 32:8

God speaks to us not only through His Word, but He also reveals Himself through our thoughts, our spirits, our conversations with others, and circumstances. If you do not currently keep a spiritual journal, I encourage you to start. It is a great way to record thoughts God brings to your mind. When I read His Word, I like writing what God is revealing to me directly into the margins of my Bible. I also keep a journal beside me to write down how He is leading me to pray. I keep a separate list of people He brings to mind. As I see the direction the Spirit is leading me to pray, I begin to get a clear idea of what He is saying to me. Then I respond in faith and obedience.

When I look back on those journals now, I see so clearly how God was preparing me! It is a faith-building blessing to see God's loving-kindness and faithful provision in our daily lives. If you look, you will see God's fingerprints in the detail of each day, whether in answered prayer or some other blessing. You will also experience His teaching,

encouragement, comfort and confirmation of His plans and purpose for your life.

As you learn to pray and listen, He will place His wants and desires into your heart. He will make His desires become your desires.

"If you are living a life that has diminished or extinguished passion, you're not living the life that God intended for you!"

— *Bob Shank, The Master's Program for Men*

Being aware of the possibility that God has a fresh calling for you will raise your awareness of His working in your daily life. Pray that God would reveal a fresh, exciting, passionate calling to you and clarify what it is!

GOD PREPARES THOSE HE CALLS

My fresh calling was to write this book, but God's calling on my life is "to bless and to heal." I began to visualize how those two ideas would come together. You see, God determines our calling, then gives us the gifts necessary to accomplish it.

God doesn't call the qualified, he qualifies the called.

— *Romans 11:29*

One day in 2010 when I was writing fast and furiously in my journal, asking God to show me what this "book of faithfulness" looked like to Him, God was reminding me my life was my story. He spoke in my heart as it quickly flowed out on paper: *"I've already given you your story, just write it."* The Father had given me a calling to bless and to heal some five years earlier when I was in my cocoon.

God gave me a passion to write and to raise up future generations of faithful children and grandchildren to impact millions.

JOURNAL: 2017

Don Jackson listened to your Holy Spirit and came to find me in Newport Beach and take me with him to his home and family in Kingsburg so both of our families would be blessed by our union. Now, being blessed with five married children and twenty-two combined grandchildren, and having this book 'placed on my heart' some seven years ago(!), the Holy Spirit has shown me what God wants to share with other women and His hurting world. As I ponder and visualize the "ripple effect" of a stone thrown into the river, I can see how the picture You gave me many years ago will be lived out in the Living Stones of all our Children and Grandchildren!

RESPONDING WITH FAITHFUL OBEDIENCE AND HUMILITY

When God gave me this fresh calling to "write a book of his faithfulness," I didn't actually begin gathering my stones for several months, because I was filled with anxiety of all sorts. I needed to place my toe in the water of the Jordan River! Only when we step out in faith will the Lord show the way. If we don't do the assignment, God will give it to someone else! He wants obedience. Faithfulness to God's call is everything.

Each of us have different callings, but all of them produce people for the Kingdom. Seeking God's direction for your life, meditating on His Word, and listening to His Spirit will bring your focus where it belongs, on Who God is and what He has called you to do.

Rejoice in the Lord always; again I will say, Rejoice.
Let your reasonableness be known to everyone.
The Lord is at hand; do not be anxious about anything;
but in everything by prayer and supplication
with thanksgiving let your requests be made known to God.
And the peace of God, which surpasses all understanding,
will guard your hearts and your minds in Christ Jesus.
Finally, brothers, whatever is true, whatever is honorable,
whatever is just, whatever is pure, whatever is lovely,
whatever is commendable, if there is any excellence,
if there is anything worthy of praise, think about these things.

— Philippians 4:4-8

As you consider your own fresh calling, allow God to redefine you and sharpen your spiritual character. Live a life of graceful obedience by the power of the Holy Spirit within you. Make wise, Scripture-based, Holy-Spirit-led choices. Pray without ceasing and seek Him and Him only. Serve the Lord for His glory and not your own.

Our spiritual life is not built in a day, but is laid daily, stone by stone. We grow in the Lord by daily discipline and acts of obedience until we love to do His will, giving all praise, honor and glory to Him. Whatever our age, He imparts what we need to be all we can be at that time. Ask God to grow your faith, as well as the faith of those you love.

Be a great person of prayer. Even if you are finished with full-time parenting or are not a parent at all, your family needs you to be a prayer warrior. The Lord already knows what we need, but when we commune with our Holy Father in Heaven, we are offering our need to Him. In turn, our love and adoration of Him develops humility, patience, and a rest in Him. Philippians 4:4-8 is one of my life verses:

GOD EMPOWERS THOSE HE CALLS

What does God desire for you? Look over the gifts and talents He has bestowed upon you. Know that God will empower you to be obedient to His call on your life! You have been set apart in this season to be God's spokesperson to all you meet through all that you do!

I propose a few questions for you to consider regarding your call:

- Is it found in God's Word?
- Does it give you indwelling peace and grace?
- Does it bring honor and glory to God?
- Does it serve others?

- Is it confirmed by others?

- Do circumstances confirm it?

- Does it create anxiety, fearfulness, and apprehension?!

That last question may be answered yes or no. Neither answer is right or wrong! Often our callings do cause anxiety we must face; sometimes they do not. All the other questions should be answered yes if you have truly received God's call.

God will supply all the wisdom, strength, and beauty of soul that you need for your fresh calling. He faithfully goes before us to give us courage to accomplish His plans. Spend time with Him so He can give you courage. Only God's Word gives life. Take advantage of this privilege!

"When you seek to perform a good work God has asked you to do, you will always find an ample supply of God's grace to sustain you... He forgives your mistakes, sets you back on your feet, and gives you the strength to continue to work."

— Experiencing God Day by Day
Devotional by Henry Blackaby, March 19

LET THE HOLY SPIRIT BE YOUR GUIDE

I originally thought I was to write one-twelfth of this story, The Lord's Love Story of Don and Jo, but the Holy Spirit had a far more beautiful idea! He guided me throughout this journey, giving me no peace whenever I was on the wrong path. Believe me, I went down plenty of rabbit holes!

He brought me just the right experience as I began writing each stone! For example, when preparing for a speaker's conference, I was assigned to write a lesson on a favorite Scripture verse. My editor and I decided to use a rough outline for this book to teach on Joshua 4. We hoped it would give us a pulse on the need for this book. I was overwhelmed with the response! From there I just got out of the way and let the Holy Spirit guide me every step of the way.

As I began writing out my journey, it was clear that my journey was most every woman's journey, though each has a different mosaic design for the stones. When sharing these ideas with my doctor at my annual checkup last year, he caught up with me again at the front desk. "You know, Jo, we men need to navigate the same stones as women." God surrounds us with His Living Waters as we navigate the stones and spiritual markers He so lovingly marks out before us. Each stone is planned and fits perfectly into His mosaic pattern for each of our lives.

My prayer is to serve the Lord in the unique way He has equipped me. I hope your prayer is the same. There is no other person created uniquely like you. God does not want us to compare our gifts with anyone else, nor are we meant to play anyone else's fiddle but our own! We are each living stones for Christ, helping to build His Kingdom people!

For we are God's workmanship,
created in Christ Jesus for good works,
which God prepared beforehand
that we should walk in them.

— Ephesians 2:10

As you come to Him, a living stone,
rejected by men but in the sight of God chosen and precious,
you, yourselves, like living stones are being built up
as a spiritual house, to be a holy priesthood,
to offer spiritual sacrifices acceptable to God through Jesus Christ.

— *1 Peter 2:4-5*

LIVING STONE MOMENTS

When I first shared these *Stones in the River* with grandchildren as they each came by, I invited them to *Join Me in The Bunkroom* to see the work of the Holy Spirit over these past two and a half years. We experienced several precious moments I like to refer to as "Living Stone Moments". To my surprise, my grandsons were just as excited for this book as my granddaughters! "I'm so excited to read your book, Grandma!" Being unsure of how the words would resonate with a boy, or young man, I would tell them, "while the subject matter is woven into a woman's journey, the book is, first and foremost, written for sharing God's faithfulness to each of you."

They were not deterred. "I know, Grandma, but you have no idea what a treasure you will be leaving with all of us."

My older granddaughters, from the fourteen-year-old on up to the married twenty-eight-year-old, mom of two, were amazed at the stones in a woman's journey. I have all twelve stones laid out in poster board outlines on three big tables in our Bunkroom. They walk in unison with me as we navigate those stones around the table.

$\mathcal{D}$o not be conformed to this world,
    but be transformed by the renewal of your mind,
that by testing you may discern what is the will of God,
    what is acceptable and perfect.

— **Romans 12:2**

"What about this stone, Grammie? What does this stone mean, Grammie? I really love this stone! Grandma, what was your favorite stone? When I grow up, Grammie, I am going to write these Stones in the River for my children and grandchildren! My favorite stone, Grandma, is the Friendship Stone, because girl friendships are really difficult in high school. I love how you've given us the 'Beautiful Face of Friendship!' I especially love Stone 10, The Lord's Love Story, because that is where I come into the book! Oh, Grandma, it will be so special to have this when I am married a long time from now. When I'm going through a difficult time, I can just pick up your book and think, 'I'll read what Grandma did when she was going through a tough time.'"

Just a week before I finished this manuscript, one of my granddaughters visited from Atlanta. We were in our favorite Fresno store, Vonda's, when we spotted an angel—not a living angel, but a beautiful wood and metal angel with a serene face. The best thing about her was that she was an angel who had "let down her wings". We stared in awe as we remembered Stone 10, when I had tried to explain to my daughters how I felt after being with Don Jackson on our first date: "I felt for the first time in ten years I could let down my wings. I felt the calm, rest, and peace of the Lord's hand upon me to 'Be still and trust.'"

We immediately bought her, had her swaddled in bubble wrap, and carried her safely home to be placed on a sofa table in the middle of the Bunkroom where she can be seen by everyone who walks through! One of my devotionals describes how angels come before the Lord and let down their wings, for only then did they hear the voice of God from the firmament above. What a beautiful reminder that we needn't be running around with our wings all raised and ruffled!

I encourage you to be intentional in creating your own Living Stone Moments with your family as you gather and write your spiritual legacy. I was amazed by how my young grandchildren grasped the metaphor of Stones in the River with the journey of life, a full life lived for God. As much as they may love reading this spiritual legacy of family stones today, I couldn't help but get a little choked up by how much more it will mean to them after the Lord has called me home. They will still be able to hear my words of encouragement and prayers for them when I am gone.

THE MAIN STONE

And now a word to my younger readers—my granddaughters and great-granddaughters, as well as others of you who are still in young womanhood, early married days, or early or middle motherhood years. The thoughts of those who are younger are often constantly pointed to the future: when you'll finish school, who you'll marry, how many children you will have, or what career you will pursue. When we're at the older end, we tend to spend a lot of time looking back over our years, often dwelling on particular seasons.

But I propose to you that whatever your age and wherever you are in your journey, the main stone is the one you are on now. The top stone is the most visible to all, the one everyone can see. The stone you are standing on right now, dear one, is your main stone.

What does God desire of you? Do you know? Or are you drifting? The stone you are now on is the one God has called you to! Embrace it, celebrate it, learn from it. Live it with excellence and exuberance!

You are writing your life story right now, one which will be read by your family, your children, your grandchildren, and your great-grandchildren. God perfectly

Every place that the sole of your foot will tread upon I have given to you,
        just as I promised Moses. From the wilderness and this Lebanon
as far as the great river, the river Euphrates, all the land of the Hittites
        to the Great Sea toward the going down of the sun shall be your territory.
No man shall be able to stand before you all the days of your life.
        Just as I was with Moses, so I will be with you. I will not leave you or forsake you.

Be strong and courageous, for you shall cause the people to inherit the land
        that I swore to their fathers to give them.
Only be strong and very courageous, being careful to do according to all the law
        that Moses my servant commanded you.
Do not turn from it to the right hand or to the left,
that you may have good success wherever you go.

This Book of the Law shall not depart from your mouth, but you shall meditate on it
        day and night, so that you may be careful to do according to all that is written in it.
For then you will make your way prosperous, and then you will have good success.

Have I not commanded you? Be strong and courageous. Do not be frightened,
        and do not be dismayed, for the LORD your God is with you wherever you go.

— **Joshua 1:3-9**

fashioned you for the place He has called you. There is no one like you, nor will there ever be! Don't miss Heaven's perspective of who you are and whose you are.

"Normally, a person will not know his or her spiritual giftedness without first receiving an assignment from God. When it is an assignment from God, you obey Him and you will see the manifestation of the Holy Spirit in new ways you have never experienced before. Focus your attention on God's call to an assignment rather than on your spiritual gifts, personal desires, personal skills, abilities, or resources.

"Once you understand God's call to an assignment, obey Him and He will work through to accomplish His purposes!"

— *Experiencing God by Henry Blackaby (73, 78)*

STEP UP TO YOUR CALL!

Dear Reader, God so clearly wanted you to have this book in your hands. I wrote it for you. It is the testimony of God's fresh calling on my life, and I can hardly wait to hear of His call for your life. Stick your toe in the water and get ready to cross the Jordan! God is calling you to courage, leadership, and obedience for your fresh calling. Answer His call. He will provide the strength, confidence, and grace to see it to fruition!

God is faithful. His footprints are all over my life story, as they are yours. I am now living my fresh calling, telling others of God's mercy, grace, love and faithfulness. I encourage you to discover your own spiritual markers, your Stones in the River to share with your children, grandchildren, and great grandchildren!

Now it's your turn! Where, oh where, Dear Reader, will your story take you?

GRACE NOTES | *A Fresh Calling*

- Pray to the Holy Spirit to reveal the talents, gifts, and character traits He has given you to use for His Kingdom. List them all in order of your years and see the common woven threads of your tapestry.

- What circumstances have shaped you and your life? What has God given you that you could use to be a blessing to others and bring them to the Kingdom? Here would be a good opportunity for you to start journaling your thoughts. Write down everything that comes to mind in prayer time. Review several areas of your life: Spiritual blessings. Family blessings. Friendship blessings. Career blessings.

- If you think your most fruitful years are behind you, remember, even as our physical bodies may slow down, our spiritual lives should be going at full speed. Making the most of The Fresh Calling stone has a way of making us productive for a lifetime—for there is no retirement for those of us in God's Kingdom. Work every day for God's glory until He calls us home.

- As a Titus 2:3-5 woman, whom can you mentor or help on the journey, using your wisdom and wholesomeness to bless and to heal?

- I love the story of Paul and Barnabas in Acts, when they were preparing themselves spiritually for whatever God might ask them to do or wherever He might send them. They "ministered to the Lord and fasted" (Acts 13:2). Are you praying and preparing for a fresh calling? When the Spirit says, "Go," will you be ready?

- When I was fearful and thinking myself totally ill equipped for this fresh calling on my life, the Spirit pressed me and reassured me He would be with me every step of the way. Do not be afraid. Do not be discouraged! Go! If God says, "Go," you need to go! He will be with you.

- Live obediently every day. "Suit up and show up." Be prepared for His orders. Remain faithful, responding with humility and obedience. Faithfulness to God's call is everything.

He is like a tree planted by streams of water.

— *Psalm 1:3*

LIVING OUT YOUR SPIRITUAL LEGACY

What have you done with the years I have given you?

What have you done with the gifts I have given you?

What have you done with the trials I have given you?

What have you done with the desert journeys I have given you?

What have you done with the resources I have given you?

What have you done with the blessings I have given you?

What have you done with My Son?

What have you done with My Holy Spirit?

What have you done with My Word?

*T*o my dear children, grandchildren, great-grandchildren, and to all of you faithful readers who have made this journey with me to the end of Stones in the River, thank you! You've heard my testimony and shared in the spiritual journey of God's love, grace, and faithfulness, navigating the stones He so carefully laid out before me, from a young girl to now. But my journey isn't done, and neither is yours! There is no kicking back and resting on past laurels. Until the Lord calls us home, there will always be an exciting life of adventure with Him. Yes, there will be more "life" as we know it, with its mountains and valleys, but I've learned the only safe place to be in my life is in His will!

And also with you! Many of you have shared this journey with me, of blood, sweat, and tears of writing "Stones," especially my husband, children, grandchildren, prayer partners, and friends! As well, there have been many of you whom the Lord brought across my path in these two and a half years of writing the manuscript, who have touched me deeply with your search for God and His Son and Holy Spirit. You have a hunger and thirst for a deeper, more intimate relationship with the Lord. Life today is transient, without roots, with little thought of who we are or where we are going. Yet, when you come face to face with the Living God, you cannot deny Him, and you want to know Him more.

Each of us is a living stone in the river of life, giving a personal testimony to Who He is, and how He came to suffer death on the cross, to rise again, and to save us from our sin, to forgive us, and give us life with Him in Heaven, for all eternity. That is the good news of Christ Jesus!

What circumstances have changed you and your life? How we navigate these stones and Who guides us makes all the difference in the world. Do we make random brush strokes across our canvas, with no thought to our choices? Or do we seek God's Word and His will for our life? God is the same yesterday, today, and tomorrow. Just as He did for Moses and Joshua and the people of Israel, He is faithful and mighty to protect and love us, and will keep His covenant with us, seeing us through our days, guiding us, caring for us, and providing for us.

One day you are going to stand before the throne of God, alone. Let your life be between you and the Holy Trinity. You will stand before God and be accountable to Him and Him alone as He asks:

> *"What have you done with the years I have given you? What have you done with the gifts I have given you? What have you done with the trials I have given you? What have you done with the desert journeys I have given you? What have your done with the resources I have given you? What have you done with the blessings I have given you? What have you done with My Son? What have you done with My Holy Spirit? What have you done with My Word?*

My dear ones, this life is preparation for our life to come with God in His Kingdom, to grow more and more like Him with every year He gives us here on earth.

How are you preparing? How are you sending it ahead? How are you sharing Jesus? How are you doing at "passing the baton" to the next generation? How are you seeking to become "Holy as I AM holy?"

Today you may be without hope. You may think you have missed the train, that it has left the station without you. You may fear it's too late for you, with nowhere to turn and no compass to find your way home. Perhaps you've never learned these "tools of life"— the knowledge and wisdom of God and His rock-solid truths.

I know there are many of you who are yearning for a closer, more intimate

As you come to Him, a living stone,
rejected by men
but in the sight of God, chosen and precious,
you yourselves like living stones
are being built up as a spiritual house,
to be a royal priesthood,
to offer spiritual sacrifices acceptable
to God through Jesus Christ.

— 1Peter 2:4-5

relationship with God, truly desirous of being a person after God's own heart. What stones do you find in your river where He was faithful in your childhood? What about the times when you were living life without a compass, unsure of your true north? Or in times of disobedience and rebellion, how He never let you go and kept pursuing you down the labyrinthian halls like the Hound of Heaven? What about your times of trial and sorrow? What about His faithfulness in your marriage when times are tough, or through the joys and challenges of raising your children?

As followers of Christ, it's good to have tangible evidence of God's help in the past. These moments remind us that His faithfulness continues today and we can follow Him with confidence into our future. We learn what's lasting and what's fading, what's urgent and what's important.

Our stones in the river are *proof of God's Faithfulness,* showing His real presence in our lives, actively giving us encouragement, strength, and hope. We can call back to one another, to those who have tired of their climb, and say, "Keep climbing!"

God is faithful, loving, forgiving, nourishing, comforting, and the Bread of Life and Living Water to our Soul!

Where are you today, child of the King? Are you alone at your Jordan? Are there decisions to be made, bills to be paid, and you don't know where to turn? Perhaps you are at the dark night of your soul. Perhaps you have lost your dream. Those of us who know Christ have resources! We have *prayer.* We have *His Word.* We have *His Holy Spirit. And Jesus, Who gives us hope.*

As a woman of God, having climbed my spiritual ladder for many decades now, there have been more rungs than I care to count when I have failed, been disobedient and rebellious, with murmuring and complaining along the climb. But I call back to you now, encouraging you on your climb to keep going!

The view gets more beautiful with every year!

God is always there, faithful to forgive us, show us unconditional love and amazing grace, as He picks us up, brushes us off, and encourages us to keep going. As husband and wife, parents, grandparents, and great-grandparents, it has been with His help that Don and I have made the passage from widowhood into remarriage, with its challenges, but, oh!, with all of its joys!

Joy and happiness are in every stone if we but look for them. Each of us could create a record of God's leading and faithfulness, reflecting on God's guidance and provision, the people, places, and experiences which are landmarks on our pathway of faith. Every remembrance of the Lord's goodness encourages us to keep walking with Him and to thank someone who influenced us for good, who stood with us in the fray, pointing our way back to the Lord, onto another stone in our river.

As I've shared my stones of remembrance for you, my children, grandchildren, and generations to come, I pray you, too, will be encouraged to keep a journal or record God's faithfulness in your Bible. Record your spiritual markers, God's call, or His intervention in your time of need. Write your journey of faith, discovery, and courage, so steadfastly guided by the Holy Spirit. Write of the truths God has revealed to you and how He works in your life. Leave a spiritual roadmap for your children and grandchildren and generations to come. Chronicle God's incredible presence during times of difficulty and disappointment, giving strength and growing your character to become more like Him.

Your chapters and seasons of life will have a different pattern than recorded here, but I trust most of us, in the end, have made or will make the same pilgrimage. The important theme in navigating these stones is God is with you through all of life. He is our mighty, sovereign Lord, whether through smooth or tumultuous waters. Your stones will be *living proof* of God's faithfulness in the past. He is there for you now. Prayerfully open your hearts and see how God is working in your life. Whichever stone you are on, you are shaping your Living Spiritual Legacy right now. We write it the way we live it out.

Live out your spiritual legacy.

God is faithful! God is mighty! God never fails us. He is shaping our character everyday, calling us into a deeper relationship with Him, preparing us for a life with Him. At times, He may go to great lengths to get our attention but nothing is ever without bringing about His purpose for our life. We have been given the command to obedience and excellence, being His hands, lips, and feet to all we meet along the way. Suit up and show up everyday to see who the Lord brings your way. Be kind, loving, and compassionate to all you meet. Give them a smile; it's amazing how it will lift their face, their countenance, and their spirit. Give them an encouraging word. We know everyone is navigating the stones in their river, as we are.

Choose to live a full life, generously using your gifts and talents for God's Kingdom work here on earth, always giving God the glory because every good and perfect gift is from Him. Live with a grateful heart, with daily expressions of "yes!" and "thank you!" to the Lord. Our life speaks to others of who we are and what we love. We may be all they know of Christ's love for them.. I pray our devotion and priority to the Lord is evident to those around us. Our life is our Living Spiritual Legacy.

I pray we will all hear,

Well done, good and faithful servant.

— *Matthew 25:21*

OUR FAMILY, 2009

Look back on your journey thus far with our faithful God. What stones are in your river of life? At the end, its the Word of God and the work of the Holy Spirit on your heart. I encourage you to *discover them, gather them, name them, embrace them, and pass them on as a living spiritual legacy of God's love, grace and faithfulness.*

Take all the Stones of your life and declare:

"This is the house that God built!"

Great Is Thy Faithfulness! Thanks Be to God!

Love and Blessings,

Jo

Logan, born 2010, and Zoey, born 2013.

...and God's story continues...

MY SPECIAL THANKS

My heart overflows with love and gratitude for all who have come alongside me on this journey. First and foremost, all praise and honor to God, my Father, Jesus Christ, my Lord and Savior, and to the Holy Spirit, whose faithfulness and presence has been with me every step of the way. I am deeply grateful for God's guidance, leading and equipping me to step out in faith and perseverance to complete this manuscript.

I thank my incredible family, beginning with my husband, Don, who intimately walked with me on this journey of discipline and obedience. Thank you for your support through all the years He told me to write it, and all the years it took me to write it! You encouraged me when I wanted to quit, loved me when I was awash with tears, endured my late hours of writing and rising before dawn to spend time in the bunkroom with God, awaiting His guidance for the Stone on which I was writing. As we both realized the intensity and immense challenge of the call, you stepped in and took over several chores, with self-made and self-completed "honey-do" lists! You did it all with a large dose of love and a cheerful, giving heart. Thank you for sharing the call.

I thank our treasured, precious daughters, Shannon and Meghan, sons-in-law, Steve and Brandon, and families, for loving, encouraging and supporting me through it all, even when you experienced first-hand, the daily time and commitment it took away from our Atlanta visits and occasions together. To our daughter, Julie, and son-in law, Ryan, to our sons Steve and Robert, and daughters-in-law, Sue and Sarah, and families in Kingsburg, thank you for your love, support and patience, along with your morning visits and uplifting prayers.

My amazing, inquiring, joyful grandchildren, you have inspired and encouraged me more times than you will ever know! Your enthusiasm and excitement for this assignment has blessed me beyond all borders! I treasure all of our "walks around the table!" I am so grateful to be your Grammie, Grandma, and "Pilgrim" in the writing of Stones. May you all take up the baton and pass on the Spiritual legacy of God's faithfulness to your children and grandchildren.

For my sister, Mary Jo, thank you for all our Monday morning talks, as you listened with your heart, offering words of love and encouragement only a treasured sister could give. Thank you for your prayers.

The stunning, beautiful book you hold in your hands is the result of three amazingly talented people.

They are all gifts from God. I am so grateful to my Editor, Bill Blankschaen, who believed in this project from the first day we met! Your literary skill and expertise helped shape the words on these pages for the glory of God. Thank you for picking me up off the floor after my occasional meltdowns. I am forever grateful for your gifted talent, patient guidance, and heartfelt prayers.

To my Graphic Designer, Margarita Capella Solazzo, you have, indeed, been blessed with God's eye for beauty and design, carrying on your father's legacy as an artist. You creatively envisioned the book from our first conversation, taking the written word and bestowing color, composition, and creativity to bring it before us as a Living Feast for the Eyes. God has given us a treasured friendship as we worked side-by-side with early mornings and late evenings these past several months. I am deeply indebted for your attention to detail, designing and redesigning, working tirelessly with purpose and pleasure for this God-given manuscript.

To my Art Photographer, Brook Todd, your visits to our home will never be forgotten. Thank you for blessing us with your eye for all things beautiful, seeing God's Hand in all that has life in His creation. Your keen sense of beauty is seen of every page of this book, presented through the lens of your camera in stunning, striking, and captivating works of art.

To my prayer sisters, Donna and Yvonne, and prayer warriors, Betty, Cheri, Dixie, Gracie, Jan, Judy, Laurie, Lavella, Pat, and Sandy, you have sustained me with your love, encouragement, and prayers. Thank you for standing in the gap and holding up my arms in the battle!

To my friend and spiritual mentor, Molly, may God bless you abundantly for the wisdom and guidance you have offered along the Stones of the way these past 30 years.

To our pastor, Scott Ardavanis, who painstakingly read every word for Biblical accuracy and application, Don and I are forever grateful. Your insight, knowledge and wisdom gave us peace and assurance in sharing God's Word. We thank you and Patty for bathing this book in prayer.

Thank you, Joni Eareckson Tada, for blessing the lives of people around the globe. Your steadfast eye on Jesus, and His hope offered for all suffering souls, inspires and challenges us all to look to the One who died on the cross for us to share eternal life with God.

May we all serve Him faithfully and with Joy! To God be the glory, now and forever!

RESOURCES

Blackaby, Henry T.

Experiencing God: Church Preparation Manual.

Memphis, TN: Brotherhood Commission, SBC, 1993.

Chambers, Oswald.

My Utmost for His Highest: Selections for the Year.

Grand Rapids, MI: Discovery House Publishers, 1935.

Cowman, Charles E.

Streams in the Desert.

Grand Rapids, MI: Zondervan Pub. House, 1965.

Elliot, Elisabeth.

Lamp Unto My Feet: The Bible's Light for Your Daily Walk.

Originally Published: Ann Arbor, MI, Vine Books, c1985.

ABOUT THE AUTHOR

Jo Jackson is an author and speaker encouraging people to recognize God's presence in their lives, and to intentionally leave a legacy of His unfailing love and faithfulness. Her passion is helping women thrive at every stage of life's journey. A former teacher, small business owner, and lover of all things beautiful, she and her beloved husband, Don Jackson, reside in Central California and Atlanta. Their greatest joy is spending time with their children, grandchildren, and great grandchildren whom they hold near and dear to their hearts. Connect with Jo Jackson at www.JoJackson.org.

W W W . J O J A C K S O N . O R G

STONES IN THE RIVER